contents

fall

trims

food

Better Homes
& Gardens

celebrate the
SEASON
2022

gifts

118 Handmade gifts send a heartfelt message. Get a jump start with clever custom-woven treasures that begin with dollar-store office accessories. Get out your button collection to make one-of-a-kind ornaments, exquisite napkin rings, button-topped gift tins, and gorgeous ribbon for wrapping extra-special gifts. Plus—delicious food gifts ready to go with the niftiest holiday presentations imaginable.

kids

138 Let mini makers join in the fun with holiday projects created just for them (but no judgement if they lure you in, too!). Check out all the professional-looking things that can be made with snow cone cups. If kids like to paint and print, this chapter offers fun ways to make cards, wrapping paper, gift tags, place mats, and more using simple items that normally go in the recycle bin.

in a twinkling

Explore quick, creative projects and recipes for impromptu get-togethers.

MEREDITH CONSUMER MARKETING
Director of Direct Marketing–Books: Daniel Fagan
Marketing Operations Manager: Max Daily
Assistant Marketing Manager: Kylie Dazzo
Content Manager: Julie Doll
Marketing Coordinator: Elizabeth Moore
Senior Production Manager: Liza Ward

WATERBURY PUBLICATIONS, INC.
Editorial Director: Lisa Kingsley
Creative Director: Ken Carlson
Associate Editor: Tricia Bergman
Associate Design Director: Doug Samuelson
Contributing Editor: Sue Banker
Contributing Copy Editor: Carrie Truesdell
Contributing Proofreader: Andrea Cooley
Contributing Food Stylist: Jennifer Peterson

BETTER HOMES & GARDENS® MAGAZINE
Editor in Chief: Stephen Orr
Executive Editor: Oma Blaise Ford
Creative Director: Jennifer D. Madara

The Greatest Gifts

I am so blessed. I am surrounded by a circle of friends who are truly the best people. Whether I need a listening ear, a date for lunch, or someone to share a laugh with, there they are, waiting to step in and brighten my spirits.

On my birthday, two of the gifts I received especially touched my heart. While every gift was treasured, these delivered a deep sense of love. The first was a beautifully handcrafted silver ring. There is an opening in the front and when looked through, my name and birthday are inscribed on the inside of the band. What a thoughtful gift that really took some planning! The other is a framed painting of wings. While absolutely stunning, it was the accompanied message that brought me to happy tears. Yes, I am truly blessed with the best of friendships.

That's how *Better Homes & Gardens Celebrate the Season* can help you. When it comes to gifts, we have the ideas and inspiration for do-it-yourself projects to touch the hearts of those you love. From woven desk accessories to some of the most delicious cookies, breads, and candies dressed up in clever handmade containers, *Celebrate the Season* offers wondrous choices. We even assist with ideas for make-it-yourself wraps and tags!

And when it comes time to start the menu planning—we have you covered! Whether gathering for brunch, lunch, or dinner, our kitchen-tested recipes offer tasty options like Spinach Pancetta Quiche (p. 93), Chipotle Chicken-Squash Chili (p. 109), and Winter Slaw with Blood Orange Vinaigrette (p. 115).

For the kiddos, there are several projects designed just for them! They will be all smiles as they display (or give away) their clever creations.

But the icing on the fruitcake is the dozens of decorating ideas waiting for you in these pages. From autumn trims to holiday treasures, you can wrap your home in a welcoming warmth that encourages beloved family and friends to stay awhile.

Be the blessing for all the special people in your life with thoughtful gifts, delicious meals, and a home overflowing with holiday cheer. These are the best gifts you can ever give, and *Celebrate the Season* is here to help!

Wishing you an unforgettable season filled with love and joy,

Sue Barker

fall

A BEAUTIFUL TIME OF YEAR
Celebrate the change of seasons with incredible decorations that share its splendidness.

Gathering Day

Make the Thanksgiving tabletop as special as the gratitude shared around it.

ON THE SURFACE

Craft a pumpkin to enjoy for many autumn seasons to come. Paint the surface of a faux pumpkin with hide glue; let dry. Paint the top half of the pumpkin with white paint and the bottom with turquoise. Let the paint dry. With just a little brown paint on the brush, paint a stripe around the pumpkin, concealing where the white and turquoise meet. Fray a strip of burlap to adorn the stem.

BRIGHT AS A FEATHER

Enhance the tabletop with paper feathers that can be crafted in minutes with minimal supplies. Cut a feather-size rectangle from tone-on-tone scrapbook paper; fold in half, long edges together. Cut a feather shape. Using fringing scissors, snip along the edge to resemble a feather. If desired, bead the center of the feather shape. Use a pin to poke a hole near each end of the feather. Cut a piece of wire 1 inch longer than the length between the holes. Bend over ½ inch on one end of the wire; insert the long end through one of the holes in the back of the feather shape. Thread the wire with seed beads. Insert the remaining wire through the front of the feather; fold over the wire end to secure.

SURFACE APPEAL
Real or faux, pumpkins gain unexpected flair with beads blanketing the skin and stem. Use straight pins to attach beads to a pumpkin. To accent the stem, thread seed beads onto wire; twist ends together to secure. Make as many beaded loops as desired. Insert the wire ends into the pumpkin near the stem. If the skin is too firm, use an awl to poke holes in the pumpkin before inserting wires.

LIGHT WITHIN LAYERS

Illuminate the glorious colors of the season with a candle surrounded by earthly tones and a pop of color. Place a short pillar candle in a round glass candleholder that allows approximately 1-inch clearance around the candle. While keeping the candle centered, gently pour a layer of popcorn kernels in the bottom of the container to cover ⅓ of the candle height. Add a thin layer of large brown seed beads. Top with a mixture of yellow, orange, green, and turquoise beads until approximately half of the candle is covered.

Never leave burning candles unattended.

WELCOME TO THE TABLE

Show guests to their spot at the table with beautiful cards marking their place. To make each place card, cut a 4×5-inch piece of white cardstock. Fold the cardstock in half, short ends together. Cut strips of decorative paper and use a glue stick to adhere them to the bottom of the place card. Use a needle and poke holes every ¼ inch along the top edge where the decorative paper meets the cardstock. Thread a needle and tape the thread end to the inside of the place card. Poke the needle through a hole at one end, thread on a seed bead, and continue sewing on seed beads through each of the holes. To add the feather accent, poke a hole on the left side of the card as shown. Bring the needle and thread through the cardstock to the top. Thread on eight large seed beads and poke the needle back through the cardstock to make a vertical line. Insert the quills of two small feathers into the top bead; hot-glue to secure if needed. Write the guest's name to the right of the feathers.

Grid Patterns

Graphic pattern play adds linear love to favorite household items and spaces.

GRID IRON

Update your throw pillows with graphic pattern by cutting a selection of colorful felt (choose three or four colors) and applying it to plain pillows. Plan a pattern, and then measure and cut felt strips. (A sharp rotary cutter, straightedge, and mat helps you make straight cuts quickly.) Cut fusible bonding web and place it between the felt and the pillow. Use a hot iron to adhere the felt to the pillow in an overlapping pattern.

Fall

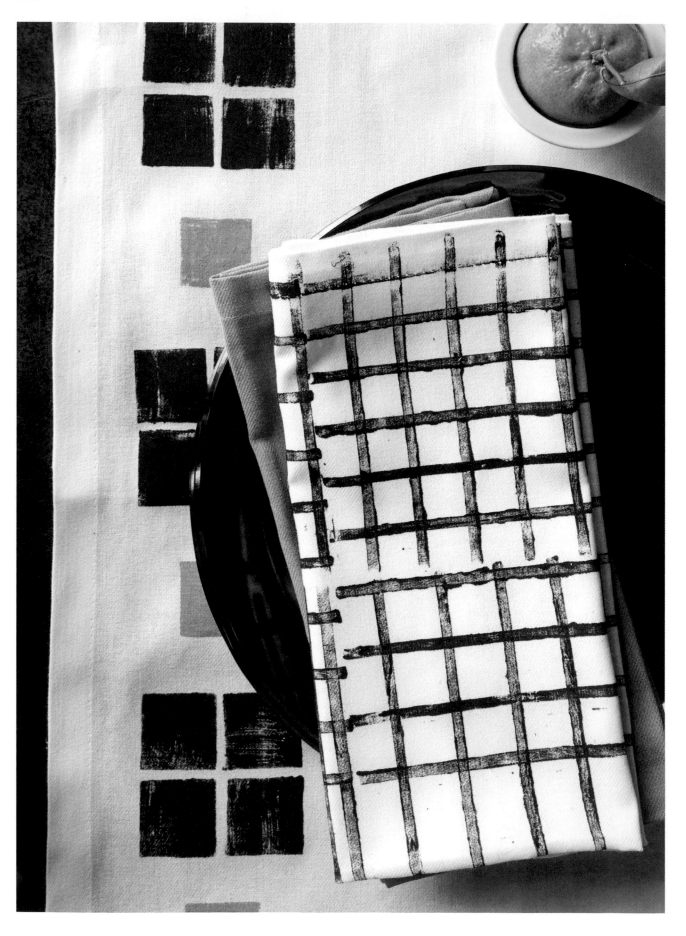

DOWN THE MIDDLE

Give a white table runner shapely feels. Press the fold lines out of the fabric to ensure a smooth surface. Measure the dimensions of your runner and plan a geometric pattern of squares, ensuring that the space between the patterns is equal. Using screen-printing ink and a paintbrush, paint the surface of a square wood block. Using even pressure, press the block into the runner and lift straight up. Measure the width to your next group of squares and repeat the process as shown in Photo A. If you're using more than one color, use a separate block for each paint.

BAND WIDTH

Your table has never looked more streamlined! After ironing a cloth napkin, place it flat on a semisoft surface such as a folded dish towel. Wrap rubber bands every inch or so around a wood block as shown in Photo B. Apply ink to the raised rubber bands using an ink roller. Lightly press the inked block to the napkin, applying even pressure. Lift straight up to reveal the linear print; allow to dry. Reapply ink to the rubber bands, rotate the block 90 degrees, and press into the napkin to create perpendicular lines.

LINEAR LOGIC

Turn elements on your nightstand from simple to striking in no time. To update a lampshade, begin by pushing a threaded needle outward from the back of the shade near the seam, about 1 inch from the bottom. Wrap the thread horizontally around the shade and insert the needle back through the original hole. Tie off the thread on the inside of the shade. Move up 1 inch and repeat the process until you have horizontal lines from top to bottom. Begin the vertical lines by pulling the threaded needle through the shade (from the inside) as close to the top as possible as shown in Photo C. Loop the thread over the top of the shade and back through the hole. Pull the thread downward and sew through the shade as close to the bottom of the shade as possible. Loop the thread around the bottom

of the shade and pull it back through the hole to tie off the thread inside the shade. Repeat every 3½ inches around the shade.

The Nature of Neutrals

Adorn your doors with one or more of these tranquil wreaths designed to extend a warm seasonal welcome.

SUPER NATURALS

Liven up traditional seasonal style with wild and unexpected botanicals. The challenge of making this natural beauty is not to overwork it. Simply form a gorgeous wreath by wiring dried foraged materials onto a grapevine base asymmetrically for a wild but modern look. No bow needed for this simple solution—a few dried flowers grouped on one side do the trick.

BOUND TO IMPRESS

Sometimes the simplest style has the biggest impact. Creating this preserved eucalyptus wreath is as easy as connecting three-stem bundles of eucalyptus together with wire and then wiring them to a 14-inch florists hoop, overlapping bunches along the way. Petite pinecones, tallow berries, and a small sprig of rosemary give the wreath added life while keeping it stylishly simple. Replace the standard bow with a natural focal point such as a cluster of larger ponderosa pinecones.

HANDMADE STYLE

Nothing says cozy quite like this creamy yarn wreath. As simple to create as it is gorgeous, this wreath requires only a few materials. Start by tying one end of a length of chunky yarn to the outside wire of a metal wreath frame. Weave the yarn over and under the parallel wires of the frame, leaving a small tail to tie on the next length of yarn. Continue tightly weaving over and under until the entire frame is covered. Wrap natural linen ribbon around the wreath to hide the yarn's starting point and provide a base for a classic tied bow. Hot-glue in place. TIP: Cut yarn into approximately two arm-lengths. The shorter pieces will be easier to weave through the frame.

WARM AND COZY

As snug as a night by the fire, this wreath gets its soft, warm aesthetic from strips of neutral plaid flannels. You can repurpose an old pair of pajamas or find myriad options at crafts and fabric stores. Simply wrap the strips around a foam wreath form, securing ends with hot glue. Add a wintry mix of faux greens to fill about a third of the wreath. Glue the flocked evergreens, pinecones, and berries in decorative groupings so the stem ends meet at a center point, leaving space for a velvet bow.

MARVELOUS MOSS

Curly dark and light Spanish moss, feathery mood moss, and lime green reindeer moss cover a straw wreath form to create a lush, carpet-like base for an assortment of pinecones. Hot-glue the pinecones facing different directions, even snuggling some in point-first, until the wreath feels full but still allows the moss to show. Tuck and glue small bunches of light pink pepperberries among the pinecones to enhance the romantic appeal.

By the Slice

Oranges, sliced into uniform wheels make a stunning presentation and preserve with ease. Simply place the slices on a parchment-lined baking sheet and bake at 200°F for 2 hours.

CITRUS AND SPICE

A simple grapevine wreath is the base for this unconventional door decoration. Begin with a layer of juniper, cedar sprigs, and magnolia leaves. Next, generously pile on dried citrus slices, overlapping and hot-gluing in place as you go. Silver brunia berries and seeded eucalyptus act as tiny ornaments, peeking above and below the translucent slices. Tie and secure bundles of cinnamon sticks with twine for the final aromatic touch.

CITRUS AND STEEL

Galvanized steel offers a spirited vibe when paired with the vibrancy of oranges. A galvanized charger hosts two coordinating gray plates. A wired vine spirals around the silver-speckled linen as a napkin ring. Dried oranges add intense color over a bed of silver dollar eucalyptus. A tag pinned to a small orange designates who sits where.

ON A ROLL

Outfit a bar cart with a charcuterie board and cocktails to get the party started. For a dash of holiday spirit, drape the cart with greenery. Create a stunning ice bucket by freezing rosemary, orange rounds, and cranberries in ice. To make it, choose a clear plastic container for the bucket and pour in 2 inches of water; freeze. Choose a smaller container that allows a 1½- to 2-inch space between the containers when centered in the bucket. Fill the small container with cold water so it doesn't float; set it in the center of the bucket. Insert rosemary, orange rounds, and cranberries in the open space between the containers, then slowly fill with cold water; freeze. Let the ice bucket thaw slightly at room temperature until the center container can be removed.

ALL IS BRIGHT

Bring out the magic of the night by dressing up shapely hurricane lanterns with rings of holiday cheer. Wire favorite greenery and white berries into a garland, or tuck in juniper berries or fresh herbs for a fragrant touch.

Never leave burning candles unattended.

Natural Beauties

Decorate for fall with displays that improve on nature. Pick up a few materials at the crafts store and on your next walk, then meld them for one-of-a-kind looks designed to last.

CAP IT OFF

Considered a symbol of good things to come, the acorn is right at home on a dining table. Personalize each place setting with a cluster of 3-D paper acorns (instructions on page 27) affixed to a twig. White gel ink on a paper-leaf place card completes the look.

PERFECT GEOMETRY

A composition of foraged objects and painted paper leaves (instructions on page 27) makes textural art. Start in the center of a mat board and work your way out using long seedpods as spokes to give the arrangement order. Hot-glue each piece in place.

BEAUTIFUL HARVEST

Paper sculptures reimagine humble staples of the season as home accents. Each squash, apple, gourd, and pear consists of eight identical pieces of folded paper. Draw inspiration from the farmers market to add distinction with painted detailing, paper-punched gourd warts, and real twig stems.

3-D PAPER SCULPTURES

Photos on pages 24, 26, 28

These artistic veggies, fruits, and gourds are sure to inspire your creativity. Made from paint-embellished paper, the shapely figures become even more interesting topped with natural stems.

WHAT YOU NEED

Patterns (see pages 150–151)
Colored cardstock
Acrylic paint
Paintbrushes
Bone folder
Transparent tape
Glue stick
Twigs
Hand pruners
Hot-glue gun

WHAT YOU DO

1. Using patterns, cut out 8 identical shapes from one color of cardstock for each structure as shown in Photo A.

2. Paint accents on paper cutouts using acrylic paint diluted with water for a soft watercolor effect. To blend colors, wet the paper first. For striations on honeynut squash, dip tip of dry flat brush into diluted paint and stroke one side of the paper.

Note: For random or allover effects, reverse Steps 1 and 2: Paint sheets of cardstock, then cut out shapes.

3. When dry, fold each cutout in half, painted side in, and press fold with bone folder. Apply glue stick to half the back of one cutout; align with back of another cutout, then press together as shown in Photo B. Repeat gluing and pressing cutouts to complete 3-D shape.

4. Use hand pruners to cut twigs for stems; hot-glue stems to top of structures as shown in Photo C. Follow the instructions for making and affixing leaves, right.

ACORNS (Pictured on page 24) No painting is needed. Cut 8 cap and base shapes from different color cardstock. Fold each cutout in half and press fold with bone folder. Tape backs of each cap and base cutout together with transparent tape. Glue, align, and press together as in Step 3.

PAPER LEAVES

Photos on pages 24, 25, 26, , 29

The shapes, folded textures, and color variety give these leaves a realistic quality.

WHAT YOU NEED

Acrylic paint
Paintbrushes
Golden yellow or green cardstock
Patterns (see page 150)
Hot-glue gun and glue sticks
Branches, vines, or twigs for stems
Florists wire

WHAT YOU DO

1. Paint accents on sheets of cardstock using acrylic paint diluted with water for a soft watercolor or spatter effect; let dry.

2. Using patterns, cut leaf shapes from painted cardstock. Fold slightly to mimic veins.

3. Hot-glue leaves to branches or bare vines, or hot-glue to florists wire, then glue wire to twigs.

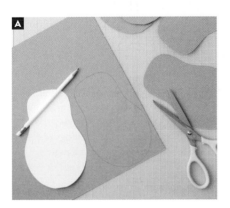

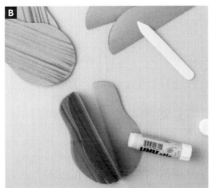

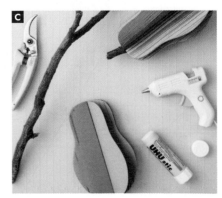

ORGANIC ORDER

Turn an assortment into a collection by grouping natural finds and crafted imitations on a tabletop. Fill cloches open-end up, cover with a piece of cardboard, then invert and slide out the cardboard.

FOLLOW THE TRAIL

To unite an assortment of pumpkins and gourds snuggled in the center of a table or lined up on a mantel, intertwine a vine. Dress up a bare vine with long-lasting leaves cut from two colors of green paper (instructions on page 27) you spatter with brown paint.

Love Live Pumpkins

Pumpkins, carved or cute, bring autumn flair and fun to your home.

SEASONAL SPLENDOR

All aglow, leaf and floral pumpkins are glorious nestled in a waterfall of gourds and uncarved pumpkins. To capture the look, cut out a hole in each pumpkin; scoop out. Use cookie cutters to impress designs into the skin of the pumpkin without going through the inside. Or, carve your own design. Use a crafts knife or pumpkin-carving tools to trim away the outer skin and membrane, leaving a layer on the inside that is approximately ¼ inch thick. Put a light on the inside of the pumpkin to make the motifs glow.

LITTLE CRITTERS

Carved eyes and beaks glow beneath owl and fox masks on these costumed pumpkins. Start by cutting holes in backs of pumpkins and hollowing out. For the masks, trace and cut out patterns, page 152, on crafts foam and affix layers with hot glue. Place masks and trace within eyes and below mask (for beaks) with a pencil; remove masks and carve features. Hot-glue masks to pumpkins. Finish by adding eye pupils glued to T-pins and inserting battery-operated lights for illumination.

Cookie Cutter Inspirations

PLEATED PLATE

A beautifully simple plate presentation turns any meal into a special event. Accordion-fold a plaid cloth napkin. Thread a chenille stem through the handle opening of a cookie cutter and use it to secure the cookie cutter around the center of the napkin. Fan out the pleats and place on the plate. Tie a ribbon bow to the chenille stem below the cookie cutter.

ALL IN A ROW

Garlands add a touch of fun and festivity wherever they hang, and this one can be created in mere minutes. Begin by tying mini cookie cutters to a length of jute string, spaced a couple inches apart. From felt, cut two narrow 4-inch strips to accent each cookie cutter. Tie the strips to the jute and trim leaving 1-inch tails. For each bow, cut a ½×5-inch piece of felt. Trim the ends to points, and tie the strip between cutters.

TO THE LETTER

Family and friends will be grateful when receiving initial cookie cutters filled with small candies in seasonal colors. To make a favor, tape cardstock to the initial, taping on the inside. Trim around the letter. Fill the shape with candy. Slip the initial into a cellophane bag; tie closed with ribbon.

CLEARLY AUTUMN

A plain glass container showcases seasonal shapes to enjoy every day of autumn. Place pinecones in the bottom of the container. Stack a few cookie cutters, placing a few pinecones in each without concealing the shapes. Tie a ribbon bow around the container base. Set a stand-up cookie cutter to one side of the container.

WAX WITHIN

Bring a soft glow to the season with candles crafted using autumn-theme cookie cutters. Using a double layer of aluminum foil, fold it up the edges of the cookie cutter, smoothing it into the creases. Set the cookie cutter in a metal cake pan. Gather autumn-color wax and a wick, or a candle. Melt wax (or candle) on the stove over low heat in a saucepan used only for crafting; remove from heat. Let set a couple of minutes, and then slowly pour the wax into the cookie cutter. Place the wick in the center of the cookie cutter; let the wax set. Place the candle on a metal plate and surround with dried putka pods.
Never leave burning candles unattended.

trims

DECORATE WITH HANDCRAFTED SENSATIONS
Create unforgettable trims and treasures to make your home a welcoming wonderland.

Tools of the Trade

Repurpose vintage tools into clever wintry sensations destined to entice wondering eyes.

GET A HANDLE ON IT

Vintage hand tools, such as files and screwdrivers, often bear ornate wood handles. These tools, whether decorative or plain, pair perfectly with wool-covered foam cones to make unique wintertime trees. To make them, choose foam cones in the desired sizes. Wrap each cone with wool fabric, leaving the exposed edge at an angle; secure with decorative upholstery tacks. Fray the exposed edge and trim the fabric even with the bottom of the cone. To secure the wood handles to a board base (this one is 6×18 inches), plan the layout and mark where each tree trunk will attach. Drill the marked areas using a ⅛-inch bit. From the bottom, insert ¾-inch #4 wood screws and tighten to the bottom of the board. Predrill each tool handle in the center, then twist them onto the screws. Attach the trees to the trunks by simply centering the top over the tool handle and pushing into place until secure.

SEE WHAT I SAW

An antiques store treasure hunt may just be the outing needed to find handsaws with vintage appeal. When selecting, look for wood handles with interesting shapes and patterns. This example shows a pair of saws that overlap so the scenes become one. Clean the saws as needed, allowing any rust to remain on the surfaces for character. Paint the desired scene (or scenes), using acrylic paint. To add a snowy appearance, dip a toothbrush into a small amount of white paint. With the bristles facing the saw, run a finger over them to fleck white dots onto the surface of each saw. To hang the saws, align the designs as desired and mark the wall through the holes at the tips of the saws. Hammer in a nail where each hole is marked.

ON THE LEVEL

An antique level in brilliant red is the perfect starting point for a clever wall-style stocking holder. To ready the level for hanging, drill a ¼-inch hole ¼ inch deep near each end on the back of the level. Choose three or four small wood knobs, matching or eclectic, to attach to the level. If desired, paint them to match the level. Use strong quick-set epoxy to attach the knobs evenly spaced on the level front.

BITS OF JOY

Time-worn rusty jumbo drill bits appear as snow-laden icicles when dusted with white paint and glitter. To make each hanger, cut a 10-inch length of brown leather lacing. Fold it in half and arrange the ends on each side of a drill bit top; secure by tightly winding wire several times around the drill bit, holding the leather hanging loop in place.

PULLEY A LA SWAG

Enhance a lovely swag by letting it flow over the top of a handsome vintage pulley. Keeping the swag simple by using a gathering of flocked greens and berries allows the 6-inch-diameter pulley to be the main attraction. A long ribbon bow adds the final polish and doubles as the hanger.

YOU KNOW THE DRILL

Sporting hand-drill antlers, this plaid reindeer is surely a prized trophy to be enjoyed all winter.

WHAT YOU NEED
Tracing paper and pencil
Scissors
Thin cardboard
2½-inch square of black felt
Plaid flannel
Instant-dry glue
Embroidery floss and needle
Cotton ball
Vintage hand drill
16×20-inch wood plaque
Drill with ⅛-inch bit
Brown cable ties
Hot-glue gun and glue sticks

WHAT TO DO

1. Trace the patterns on page 155; cut out shapes. Use the patterns to cut two ears, one head, and two side pieces from thin cardboard. Cut one nose from black felt; set aside nose.

2. Lay the cardboard shapes on the wrong side of the plaid flannel, placing so the plaids align when sewn together. Cut the flannel ½ inch beyond the cardboard. Cut a second set of ears.

3. With the wrong side of the flannel on top of the heads and sides of cardboard shapes, hand-press the excess flannel to the back. Turn over each piece and glue the excess fabric to the back. Attach one side piece to the center head piece using embroidery thread and hem stitches. Repeat for the other side piece. Hem-stitch around the outer edge.

4. For each ear, align two flannel shapes with right sides facing. Hand-stitch the layers together, ¼ inch from the edge, using running stitches; leave the straight ends open. Clip the corners and turn right side out. Bending the cardboard as needed, slip an ear shape into each ear piece (rolling as needed to fit through the open end). Outline each ear with hemstitches sewn only through the top layer of flannel.

5. Sew the nose to the head piece using running stitches. After stitching around half of the nose, tuck in the cotton ball. Continue stitching closed.

6. Arrange the drill and head pieces on the plaque. Mark sets of holes where the drill will best attach to the plaque, spacing each set ½ inch apart. Remove all pieces and drill holes where marked. Attach the drill antlers using cable ties, securing on the back of the plaque; cut off the excess.

7. Use hot glue to attach the head to the plaque, positioning so the drill appears to rest on the head piece. Glue each ear in place, tucking slightly under the head piece to hide the ends.

Deflated and Elated

No need to inflate the balloons used for these joyful decorations—they are perfect just as they are.

HEAVENLY CHERUB

Layered with texture, color, and meaning, this angel welcomes in the spirit of the season.

WHAT YOU NEED
Yellow water balloons
Foam cone
Map pins in yellow and white
Scissors
9-inch balloons in pink and gold
2½-inch foam ball
Black fine-tip marking pen
3 toothpicks
Chenille stem in white or yellow
Long balloons in yellow and white
Tracing paper and pencil
⅛-inch-thick foamcore board
Straight pins

WHAT YOU DO
1. Starting at the base of the cone, pin yellow balloons, slightly above the rounded end, around the cone's base. Continue adding balloons in this method, working upward in rings, until the entire cone is covered.
2. Snip off the end of a pink balloon. Place a white map pin in the center of the foam ball for the nose. Stretch the balloon over the foam ball and nose, adjusting so the balloon opening is at the top with the nose remaining in the center.
3. Using the marking pen, draw eyes as shown while keeping the nose as the center point.
4. Knot the open end of the gold balloon for a ponytail. Cut off the rounded end of the balloon. Pull the gold balloon over the pink balloon; cut as desired for the angel's hair. Snip the balloon as desired to fringe the hair ends and the ponytail.
5. Press the three toothpicks into the top of the cone, spacing slightly apart. Push the head onto the toothpicks.
6. Trace the wing pattern on page 157. Use the pattern to cut wings from foamcore. Beginning at the outer edge, pin the rounded tip of a white balloon to the end of the foamcore. Stretch the balloon toward the wing center, secure in place with a straight pin inserted lengthwise into the foamcore to conceal the sharp point. Continue adding white balloons in this manner until the wings are covered as shown in Photo A.
7. Cut a 7-inch-long piece of chenille stem. Cut off the opening end of a yellow balloon, leaving 7 inches. Insert the chenille stem into the balloon, and attach to the angel head, pinning the ends together in the back as shown in Photo B.
8. Pin the wings to the back of the angel, placing so that the top of the wings are approximately ½ inch below the angel's head as shown in Photo B.

TREE OF GREENS

A variety of green balloons, even some polka-dotted, join together to make a whimsical tabletop tree. Start with a 12-inch-tall foam cone. Working from the bottom to the top, attach balloons to the cone using map pins. For the topper, tie off the ends of several red and yellow water balloons. (Note: If desired blow a puff of air into each before tying.) Pin the mini balloons to the top of the foam cone. Surround the tree with mini packages, and the tree becomes a magical centerpiece.

PACKAGE POINSETTIA

Chenille stems give this package topper long-lasting shape. To make eight red poinsettia petals, bend a yellow or green chenille stem in half and insert into each balloon; allow the chenille stems ends to poke out from the balloon. Pulling the chenille stems outward, shape the poinsettia petals. Gather the balloons, chenille stems up, and wrap tightly with a red chenille stem approximately ½ inch from the balloon ends. Twist the chenille stem ends together to secure, and cut off the excess. For the flower center, thread a small yellow or green wood bead onto the end of each corresponding chenille stem. Shape the chenille stems to wrap once around each bead.

MERRY AND BRIGHT

A hard plastic ornament offers limitless design potential with bands of balloons coating its surface. Cut a variety of band widths from various colors of balloons. Stretch the bands to cover the ornament shape, overlapping if desired.

DRESSED TO CHILL

All decked out for the chilly season, this fella's smile is contagious. To make the ornament, cut off the open end of a white balloon; stretch over a 2½-inch foam ball. Using a purple-and-white polka-dot balloon, cut off the open end. Pull the hat piece over the top of the head to cover approximately one-third of the face. To make the solid purple cap accent, cut a ½-inch strip from a balloon using pinking shears. Pull the ring over the cap, arranging it to cover the bottom of the cap. For eyebrows, use pinking shears to cut off the ring end of the white balloon; cut in half. To make a scarf, cut a long strip from a green balloon; fringe the ends. Use a black marking pen to draw in the eyes and mouth. Use instant glue to attach the eyebrows and an orange bead nose to the snowman. For the hat accent, cut off the ring end of a green balloon. Attach it to the hat using three red map pins. To hang, poke a wire hanger through the top of the hat.

CHEERY ST. NICK

Let the magical man of the hour add a playful touch to Christmas tree branches. Cut off the open end of a pink balloon; stretch over a 2½-inch foam ball. Cut off 1 inch from the end of a white balloon; set aside. With the end of the pink balloon down, pull the white balloon over the pink, approximately one-third up the foam ball to resemble a beard. Using a red balloon, knot the opening and cut off the rounded end. Pull the hat piece over the top of the head to cover approximately one-third of the face. To make white cap accent, cut off a ½-inch scalloped strip from the set-aside white balloon. Pull the ring over the cap, arranging it to cover the bottom of the cap. For eyebrows, use pinking shears to cut off the ring end of the white balloon; cut in half. Use pinking shears to cut a mustache shape from the white balloon. Use a black marking pen to draw in eyes. Use instant glue to attach the eyebrows as well as the mustache and a bead nose to St. Nick. To hang, poke a wire hanger into the knot at the top of the hat.

Icy Wonders

Joy to the world and all its natural beauty! These projects freeze some of nature's finest treasures to behold until they melt with the warmer days of spring.

NOTHING BUNDT HOLLY

Showcase a seasonal favorite nested in a glistening, see-through wreath. To make the ring, fill a Bundt pan three-fourths full of ice-cold water. Arrange holly clippings, along with berries, into the water and let it freeze. Release the frozen ring by setting at room temperature until slightly melted or by running water over the mold. Hang the elegant ring from wire-edged ribbon outside.

SEASONAL PRESERVATION

Dried flowers saved from your garden or a fresh flower delivery, infuse wintry ice disks with luscious color. Choose a round cake pan in the desired size; fill with water. Sprinkle dried flowers into the water. Add snippets of greenery. Cut a 36-inch piece of twine; fold in half. Place the loop of the twine into the water as a hanger. Let the arrangement freeze, and hang outside near a window to enjoy.

ORANGE JUBILEE

Include bird friends during the season of giving with edible delights hanging in the yard. Cut slices and wedges from an orange. Arrange the orange pieces and blueberries in a small cake pan; cover with water and let freeze. To release the frozen treats from the pan, let set at room temperature or run water over the pan for a few seconds. To hang, cut two 36-inch lengths from jute; knot together in the center. Arrange the jute ends in a plus and set the frozen circle in the center. Bring up the jute ends; and knot them together. Hang the feeder, keeping the frozen shape as level as possible.

FOR THE BIRDS

So pretty as suncatchers, and even more alluring with birds flocking about, these fruity ice shapes liven up the yard. Ice cube trays for bottles and muffin tins make fun shapes for the birds to flock to. Arrange oranges and blueberries in the molds, then add water and lengths of jute for hangers; allow to freeze. Remove the frozen shapes and hang outside.

FIRE AND ICE

Enjoy the glow of candles as they flicker amidst an icy ring of greenery snippets and mini pinecones, above. To make the arrangement, place eight tea candles in a large round cake pan. Arrange the candles in a small inner circle and add one candle in the center. Cut pieces of greenery and sprinkle around the candles. Add mini pinecones to the arrangement. Pour in just enough water to let the adornments freeze to the bottom of the pan; place in freezer or outside if the temperature is below freezing. Once frozen, fill the pan with ice-cold water and let freeze. To remove the decoration, let set at room temperature until it loosens from pan. Please note that it may be hard to keep candles lit outdoors due to wind. You may want to replace the candles with battery-operated ones once the ring is frozen. To make an interesting suncatcher using this method, simply remove the candles once the piece is frozen and hang the piece from ribbon threaded through one of the openings, right.

Never leave burning candles unattended.

Americana Christmas

Salute the red, white, and blue with celebratory trims and tokens of love.

BEADED BAUBLES

Wood beads in red, natural, and blue tones join together to make super-simple ornaments. To make one, cut a 16-inch length of red-and-white string. Wrap one end of the string with tape to allow easy stringing. Determine the order of the beads. Starting with the top bead, thread them onto the taped end of string. When the last bead is attached, arrange beads so that the bottom bead is in the center of the string. Thread the string through the next bead and continue in this manner until the string is threaded back through the first bead. Knot the string ends; clip off the tape.

RED AND WHITE AND BLUE ALL OVER

Decorative party picks become tree-ready ornaments with the easy addition of a handful of wooden beads. Choose sparkly picks in a patriotic color. On the wood end, thread on wood beads in the desired pattern. Hot-glue the final bead in place to secure the beads from falling off. Add a hanger by threading string though a loop on the pick top. If there are not loops, use a dot of hot glue to attach the hanger.

WREATH OF HONOR

A traditional wreath takes a patriotic turn with its distinct color scheme and flaglike focal point. Wire pinecones and ball ornaments in reds, blues, and silver to a large fresh or faux wreath. Wire two jumbo peppermint sticks together in the center. Arrange the sticks into an X and attach to the wreath. Accent the center with a piece of cording.

MEDALLION OF HONOR

Trim the tree with showy paper-and-bead medallions that come together easily using red-and-white striped baking cups. To make a medallion, start with a 4-inch pleated baking cup. Measure and mark four equally spaced spots ¼ inch in from the top edge. Use a needle to poke through where marked. Cut a 4-inch circle from silver paper and adhere it inside the baking cup using clear double-sided tape. Poke a hole in the center of the paper. Thread a needle with blue embroidery floss, knotting one end. From the back of the cup, poke the needle through the hole, slip on a ¼-inch red wood bead, and poke the needle back through the hole. Fold over the cup edge where one of the holes was pre-poked. Use the hole as a guide to poke a hole through the silver and paper and bottom of the cup. From the back side of the cup, bring the needle to the front, being sure to go through the pre-poked hole along the cup edge. Thread on three ¼-inch blue wood beads, insert the needle next to the red bead, and pull through to the back. Continue adding blue beads in this manner until there are four spokes as shown. Cut a 20-inch length of ½-inch-wide blue velvet ribbon; fold in half. Leaving 2-inch tails, hot-glue the ribbon to the back of the ornament. Thread a 1-inch red wood bead through the ribbon hanging loop. Trim the ribbon ends to points as shown. Cut a 3½-inch circle from silver paper; secure it on the back using double-sided tape.

COOL SPOOL

A large spool of red-and-white string becomes a fun starting point for a miniature holiday scene. Holding true to patriotic colors, choose bases for the tiny bottlebrush trees such as miniature spools or wood beads. Hot-glue the bases to the large spool top, stacking items if desired for the focal tree. For an eye-catching accent, trim the main tree base with string from the spool. Remove the trees from their original bases by twisting them apart; hot-glue each tree atop its new base. Glue on small bead tree toppers as desired. A single tree set on the surface completes the display.

SWEET SERVINGS

Cups created for Independence Day take on a Christmassy vibe with the use of candy canes and seasonal silvery picks. Fill each cup with treats, the pick, and candy canes in red, white, and blue. Tie a small red-and-white string bow and hot-glue it to the rim.

LBS. NET
KILOS

Brown's
Best

CHESTER B. BROWN CO.
IDAHO 83350
OFFICE - MORRILL, NEBR.
PRODUCT OF U.S.A.

Old-Fashioned Flair

A stroll through the antiques store while keeping an open imagination can uncover extraordinary finds for holiday decorating. Be on the lookout for items in your color scheme. Then, with just a few simple additions, transform the items into the finest Christmassy trims.

STITCHES AND A SACK

A feed sack in seasonal colors lends vintage appeal to the table. To make a table runner, cut the bag down the sides and across the bottom. Choose which side you wish to use; fray each side. Enhance the printed design with embroidery stitches using floss that coordinates with the print. For stitch diagrams, see page 154.

SELF-CONTAINED

Antique tins make fascinating containers for small holiday arrangements. Using an empty, clean container, tuck in small faux holiday picks. For a fresh arrangement, put a little water in the tin, then add the desired greenery, berries, and small flowers.

YULE SPOOLS

Welcome guests to the table with mini decorations set beside each place card. To make a spool decoration, hot-glue a snippet of faux greenery in one end of a wood spool. Affix a tiny pinecone and faux berries on the top. To make the adornments look snowy, brush them with a small amount of white paint. If the spool is empty, wrap it with a short length of embroidery floss in a holiday hue.

Festive Place Settings

Imagination—and a little craftiness—is all it takes to surprise those gathering at the table with thoughtful place settings.

TRUCK STOP

A red toy truck delivers sweet treats and holiday cheer. To dress the truck in seasonal style, hot-glue a miniature wreath to the front grill and a bottlebrush tree to the truck bed. Place wrapped candies in the truck bed.

YULE LOG

A beautiful nod to nature, this pretty display brings cozy warmth to the dining table. Using a half round of a short birch log, saw a ⅛-inch slit along the top of the log. Make a layered paper name tag; slip into the slot. Tie a multi-ribbon bow from ¼-inch plaid ribbons; hot-glue to the log. Add a trio of pinecones and dust with white paint if desired.

CUP-O-PLENTY

For a last-minute sensation, place a sweet or salty treat into a cellophane treat bag; tie closed with ribbon. Place the bag into a cup for a surprise that serves two gifts in one.

COOL PRESENTATION

This fun-loving place setting is all about placement. With a white dinner plate center stage, tuck a cloth napkin or towel under the bottom lip of the plate and pull to one side to resemble a scarf. To make the hat, fold a fabric napkin in half point to point. Fold up a 2-inch brim. Place the brim over the top of the plate; fold under the sides. Tuck the tableware under the brim. Use a cup for the pom-pom. For the face, use black jelly beans for the eyes and smile and an orange slice for the nose. Complete the look with an oversize wood fork.

A Way with Clay

Easy to roll, impress, twist, and paint, there's everything to love about oven-bake clay.

DOVE OF PEACE

Soft and calm, or bold and bright—this ornament has endless finishing options.

WHAT YOU NEED
White oven-bake clay
Waxed paper
Tracing paper and pencil (optional)
Hobby knife
Paperclip
Crochet hook
Straw
Awl
Brush-style clay tool
Comb-style clay tool
Acrylic paint and paintbrush
String

WHAT YOU DO

1. Place a chunk of white clay on waxed paper as shown in Photo A. Place another piece of waxed paper on top and flatten to ¼ inch using a rolling pin as shown in Photo B. Remove the top layer of waxed paper.

2. Freehand-cut a bird shape and wing shape as shown, or use the pattern on page 154 to cut your shape. Use a hobby knife to cut away excess clay as shown in Photo C.

3. Fold open a paperclip and use it to impress scallops along the bottom edge of the bird as shown in Photo D.

4. Using a crochet hook, impress the clay between the scallops and the wing as shown in Photo E.

5. For the eye, press the straw into the clay. Dot the center using an awl. For the eyelashes, use the tip of a hobby knife to impress them above and below the eye as shown in Photo F.

6. Press a thumb into the clay where the wing will attach as shown in Photo G. Place the wing into the indentation as shown in Photo H.

7. Use a brush-like clay tool to make dotted impressions on the wing as shown in Photo I. Press the tip of a knife into the wing edge to create small triangles along the edge as shown in Photo J.

8. For the tail feathers, press the knife tip into the clay to make small Vs as shown in Photo K.

9. Use a straight comb-like clay tool to make a dotted line like a comb as shown in Photo L.

10. Accentuate the beak if desired. Use the awl to make a hole near the top of the wing for hanging.

11. Following the manufacturer's instructions, bake the clay bird in the oven. Remove from oven and let cool.

12. Using acrylic paints of your choosing, paint the sections of the bird; let dry. For the hanger, thread string through the hole in the wing; knot the ends and trim off excess.

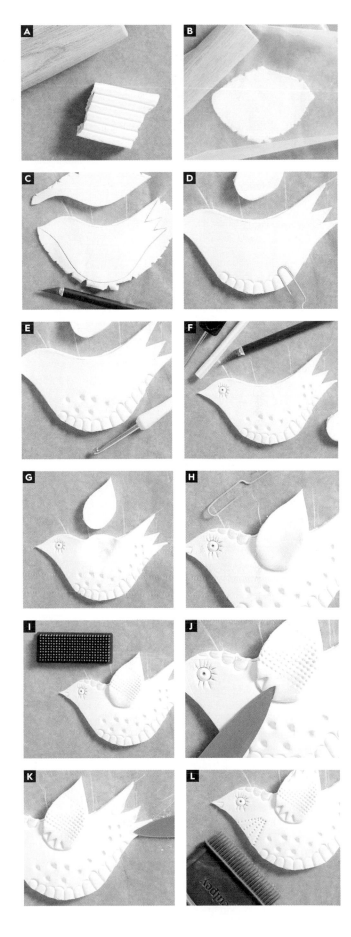

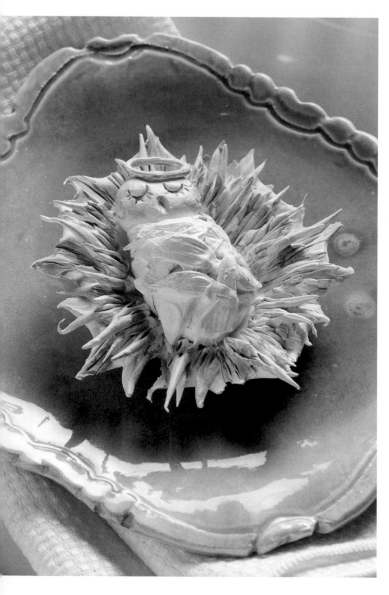

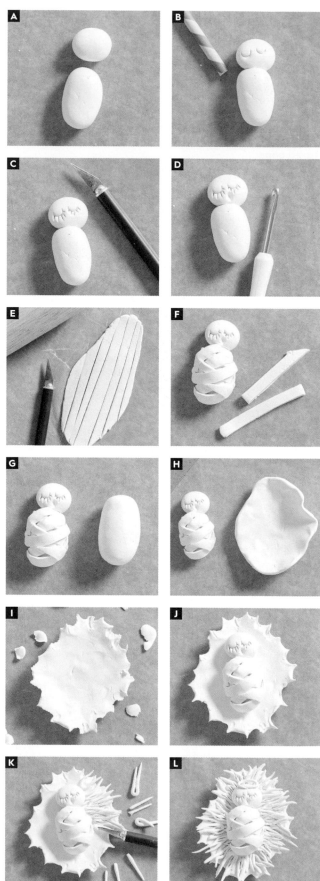

CRADLE OF HOPE

Sculpt your own rendition of baby Jesus asleep in the hay. Roll an oval piece of white oven-bake clay for the head and a larger one for the body as shown in Photo A. Press the clay pieces together. Use the edge of a straw to make U-shape eyes as shown in Photo B. Add lashes below each eye by pressing a hobby knife into the surface as shown in Photo C. Add a mouth by pressing the tip of a crochet hook into the clay head as shown in Photo D. Roll a piece of clay flat and slice narrow strips as shown in Photo E. Use the strips to wrap the baby's body as shown in Photo F. Roll an oval from clay approximately the size of the baby as shown in Photo G. Press the oval into an irregular oval cupped shape as shown in Photo H. Pull away tiny pieces from the edge of the oval as shown in Photo I. Place the baby in the center of the oval as shown in Photo J. Roll tiny clay spikes for hay and press onto the baby's bed using a crafts knife as shown in Photo K. Continue adding hay until the baby is surrounded as shown in Photo L. Following the manufacturer's instructions, bake the clay piece in the oven. When done, remove from oven and let cool. Using a small amount of watered-down acrylic paint, paint the baby, halo, and the bed of hay.

LIGHT OF HAPPINESS

From white oven-bake clay, roll approximately 26 small straw-size pieces long enough to cover a round glass candleholder top to bottom as shown in Photo A. Holding two clay ropes side by side, twist the pieces together as shown in Photo B. Continue twisting, alternating the direction in which the pieces are twisted. Lay two twisted clay pieces side by side as shown in Photo C. Press the pieces gently together, them press gently onto the surface of the candleholder. Once the candleholder is covered, trim off the excess clay with a hobby knife. For rim: Twist together two ropes long enough trim the rim; press into place. Following the manufacturer's instructions, bake the clay piece in the oven. When done, remove from oven and let cool. Using a small amount of watered-down acrylic paint, brush the surface of the candleholder. Let the paint dry. Insert a candle into the holder.

Never leave burning candles unattended.

FLAKES OF JOY

Just like the real thing, each one of these dainty beauties is different than the rest. To make snowflake ornaments, roll oven-bake clay between two pieces of waxed paper until ¼ inch thick as shown in Photo A. Remove the top layer of paper and use a cookie cutter to make a snowflake shape as shown in Photo B. If desired, use smaller snowflake cookie cutters to gently press designs into the surface of the clay cutout as shown in Photo C. To add circles, use a straw as shown in Photo D. Make a hole in the top of the snowflake for hanging. Following the manufacturer's instructions, bake the clay piece in the oven. When done, remove from oven and let cool. Using a small amount of watered-down acrylic paint, brush the surface of the snowflake. Let the paint dry. Insert a string through the hole for hanging.

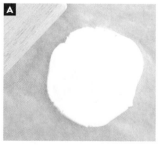

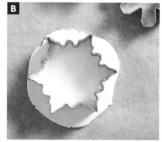

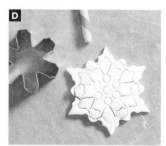

HOUSE OF LOVE

Whether you craft a cute little cottage or a replica of your own home sweet home, using oven-bake clay opens the door to all kinds of creative possibilities. To make the cottage, place a chunk of oven-bake white clay on waxed paper. Place another piece of waxed paper on top and flatten to ¼ inch using a rolling pin. Remove the top layer of waxed paper. Using a crafts knife, cut a 2¼-inch square for the house and a triangular roof, see pattern on page 154. Cut out a ½-inch square window on the right side of the house. Flatten a tiny bit of clay to approximately ⅟₁₆ inch thick; gently smooth onto the back side, covering the window opening. Use an opened paper clip to impress the roof and door. Use a crafts knife to make horizontal lines on the house, vertical lines on the doors, and a crossbar in the window. Roll tiny icicles, greenery, and berries from clay, press on to the roofline and windowsill. Following the manufacturer's instructions, bake the clay and let cool. Using watered-down acrylic paints in the desired colors, paint the house; let dry. For the hanger, thread string through the hole and knot the ends.

Oh Night Divine

The true meaning of the season is captured in these radiant designs, reminding us of the promise of hope, peace, and love.

WE THREE KINGS

Attired to behold the sight of the newborn King, no one would know these Wise Men take their basic shapes from spray bottles rescued from the recycle bin.

WHAT YOU NEED

3 spray bottles in the shape shown in Photo A, with the sprayer discarded
Yarns in jewel tones
Scissors
Hot-glue gun and glue sticks
Assorted gold trims
Tracing paper and pencil
Felt in jewel tones
Three 1½-inch wood balls for heads
3 bottle caps
Three 1¼-inch lids for crowns
Gem stickers

WHAT TO DO

1. To make the Wise Men with short cloaks, start by wrapping bottles with yarn. Hot-glue one end to the base and wind upward, tacking with glue as needed. Accent each base with gold trims.
2. Trace the patterns on page 153; cut out. Use the cloak pattern to cut the shapes from the desired color of felt.
3. Hot-glue the short cloaks to the yarn-wrapped figures as shown, folding over a collar at the top. For the long-cloaked figure, glue a felt piece to the base, a short-cloak cutout to the front of the figure, and the long cloak to the back, folding over the collar as shown.
4. For the heads, hot-glue a wood ball to each spray bottle opening.
5. For each Wise Man, cut a 1×4-inch piece of felt to wrap the neck; glue into place.
6. For crowns, hot-glue a bottle cap atop each lid. Spray-paint the crowns gold; let dry. Hot-glue a crown on each Wise Man's head.
7. Use your imagination to add scarves of yarn or felt to the figures. Decorate the clothing and crowns with trims, gems, and felt as desired. For the short cloak side motif, see the patterns on page 153.

A

ROYAL BEAUTY BRIGHT
Grace the edge of a gold plate charger with brilliant adhesive gemstones pressed into place. If desired, make a mirror-image design or an eclectic one. When planning the design, keep in mind the size of plate to be set on the charger so the gorgeous edge is allowed to shine.

BEJEWELED ORNAMENT
A gold plastic ornament gets the royal treatment with the addition of sparkling gem stickers. Decorate the ornament as you wish, covering just the front, the top, a ring around the center, or the entire surface. As long as the ornament is plastic (not glass), this project is a great one to make with kids.

GIFTS OF GOLD

Keep the theme rolling with elegant crown candy favors, rich in color and texture. Trace the crown patterns on page 152; cut out. Use the patterns to cut crown shapes from decorative gold cardstock. Using an empty water bottle or similar straight-sided plastic container, cut off 2 inches from the bottom of the base. Wrap the crown piece around a cup; hold in place with double-sided tape. Add desired gold trims around base. Accent crown front with gem stickers and additional trims. Place candies in a cellophane bag; tie closed with a wire twist tie.

STAR OF WONDER

Glistening with royal beauty bright, this gem-studded card is sure to delight its recipient. Trace the pattern on page 152; cut out. Use the pattern to cut a star shape from gold paper. Use a glue stick to adhere it to black paper; trim a narrow border. Use a 1-inch punch to make the center circle from gold marbled paper; adhere it to the center using a glue stick. Use the marble paper to accent each star point by cutting the same shape as the star, then trimming off ⅛ inch from the outer edge and cutting off the points with straight cuts to leave approximately ¼ inch free around the center circle. Glue the triangles to the star points. Glue the star to a 3½×4¾-inch piece of white cardstock. Glue to black paper and trim a narrow border. Glue the layers to the front of a 4¼×5½-inch colored notecard. Use gem stickers to accent the star.

GUIDING LIGHT

Simple cardstock place cards get a majestic nudge with the addition of star charms pinned to the front. Cut a 4×4½-inch piece of decorative gold cardstock; fold in half with long edges together. Cut a 4×1-inch piece of white cardstock; adhere to front of place card using double-sided tape. Write the guest's name on the card. Attach a gold star charm to the front of each card, pinning in place using a pearl-head corsage pin.

Beads All Around

Wood beads, available in several sizes and colors, make holiday crafting easy-peasy peppermint squeezy.

RING OF BEAUTY

Whether used as an ornament, package trim, stand-alone decoration, or something else, this mini wreath is as cute as it is easy to make. Cut three 12-inch lengths of wire. With ends even, thread on a medium-size green wood bead, slide it about 1 inch from the end, and bend the wires up to hold the bead in place. Separate the wires and thread each with a small green, red, or bright pink bead. Continue beading in this manner until the wires are filled with beads; twist the wire ends together. Tie a double bow at the top with ¼-inch-wide ribbons and a single ribbon for the hanger.

TO HAVE AND TO HOLD

Display holiday cards like artwork, clipping them on a pretty beaded garland for everyone to enjoy. To make stringing the wood beads easy, use leather cording, as it is firm enough to thread on beads without the use of a needle. Cut the cord into the desired length and thread on beads, in a pattern, until the desired length is achieved. This bright garland uses two sizes of wood beads and seven colors. For another color variation, see the book cover for a more traditional rendition. To hang the cards, snap on vinyl badge clips where desired (see Photo A).

A

FILLED WITH CHARACTER

Perched on a live-edge wood slice, this miniature snowman is a real charmer. To make him, hot-glue a 1-inch wood ball inside the opening of a 1¼-inch wood bead. Glue the bottom of the snowman to a ¾-inch donut-style bead. Paint the entire figure white; let dry. For the hat, hot-glue a ¼-inch wood plug inside a second ¾-inch donut-style bead. Paint the hat black; let dry. Glue the hat to the snowman, positioning it slightly to the back. Glue a tiny orange wood bead to the center of the face. Paint the snowman's smile by dipping the end of a toothpick into black paint and dotting it on the surface. To paint the eyes,

place more paint on the toothpick and dot onto the face. Cut several colorful fibers and tie around the neck for a scarf, trimming the ends if needed. Hot-glue a single fiber around the hat brim. To make the trees, hot-glue ¾-inch wood disks to the bottom of miniature wood spools. Paint the bases red; let dry. Working with one at a time, fill the opening in the spool with hot glue and insert a toothpick. Repeat for each spool. Thread the toothpicks with graduating sizes of wood beads. Hot-glue a small yellow bead to each top. If the toothpick shows at the top, paint it with bright yellow to match the bead; let dry.

Good Tidings

Spread joy to the world by creating miniature magical moments from a few of your favorite holiday things.

O CHRISTMAS WREATHS

Make the season bright by gathering petite wreaths made from evergreens and dried herbs. Attach cut greens, berries, and pinecones to wire forms and 3- to 5-inch embroidery hoops using florists wire and hot glue. Leave some embroidery hoops partially exposed for an airy look. Hang wreaths from lengths of ribbon or rickrack at different heights to festively display your verdant rings.

LOVE AND JOY

Create a merry tabletop with a simple, joyful centerpiece. Lay seeded eucalyptus, pinecones, and hypericum berries on a plate or charger with a decorative rim. Fill a trio of vintage milk bottles or glass vases with evergreen branches and white and red berry sprigs that will last into the happy new year. Change water daily to keep live greens fresh and fragrant.

SILVER BELLS

Dress mint julep cups and silver bowls in red-and-green finery for holiday style. Let them ring-a-ling by filling each one three-fourths full with marbles, then adding green reindeer moss and sprigs of highbush cranberries or hypericum berries. Finally, nestle glass votive candles inside, making sure each candle stands above the moss and berries. Arrange on a silver tray or platter to celebrate that soon it will be Christmas day.

HOLLY JOLLY

Toast your favorite ornaments with a cup of cheer by dressing up a cupboard or buffet with a festooned garland. Made from sturdy twigs painted white, the garland is held strategically in place with clear pushpins. Hang a mix of ornaments in different sizes and colors. Complete the look by tucking in fresh or faux greens, and you're ready for the best time of the year.

BE OF GOOD CHEER

Tie treasured or found ice skates to a banister or door for a playful touch. Stuff skates with tissue paper to keep boots firm and shapely. Top with fresh greens, then hang a few vintage ornaments over each skate's top for a dash of holiday panache. Tie in place using long ribbon for laces.

New Year Celebration

As a brand-new year unfolds, embrace your creativity—starting with party decorations to share with family and friends.

A SIGN OF THE TIMES

Make a big impact with little effort by creating a banner to set the tone of the party. Print "CHEERS" using a 350-point font, printing each letter centered on a separate page. Use the triangle pattern on page 155 to cut out the letters. Place each letter on turquoise cardstock or cardboard; cut around triangle leaving a ½-inch border. Use a paper punch to make a hole at the top tips of each triangle. Starting from the front side, thread ¼-inch ribbon into the C letter banner. Continue adding letters in this method until CHEERS is spelled out.

TOASTING TOP HATS

Offer guests their favorite libations nested cheerfully in a paper top hat. To make a hat, cut a 3½-inch section from a toilet paper tube. Cover the tube with black glitter paper using double-sided tape. Cut a 3-inch circle and hot-glue the tube in the center. Trim the hat with gold glitter ribbon and pom-pom berries. Print out "CHEERS TO THE NEW YEAR" on white paper, stacking the words as shown to make the banner approximately ¾×1½ inches. Cut out the message using pinking shears. Shape the message as shown; hot-glue to the hat by the berries. Fill the hat with a piece of gold garland and set a single-serving bottle inside.

SWEET MUSIC

Gift your fellow party people with noisemakers holding celebration candies inside. When the clock strikes midnight, set aside the cellophane piping bag of treats and let the noisemaking begin!

TIMELY TABLE MARKERS

Set where you wish, these glittery papers deliver individual messages of cheer. Cut a 4×8-inch piece of glitter paper; fold in half with the short ends together. For the message, cut a 4×1¼-inch piece of glitter paper. Using a computer and printer, print several "Happy New Year!" messages, each to fit a 3¾×1-inch rectangle. Cut out the messages. Adhere each message to a background piece using double-stick tape; tape to card front where shown. Use circle punches to make circles from different colors of glitter paper. Use a glue stick to adhere the circles, some layered, to the place card front.

COLOR-BURST FIREWORKS

Craft festive tabletop bursts that can be made in any color. Using toothpicks pointed on both ends, poke one end into a 1-inch foam ball until the spikes extend in every direction. In a well-ventilated work area, spray-paint the spheres with metallic paint; let dry.

TREAT TOPPERS

Party hats are a must for New Year's Eve celebrations and party pics. And while these were ready to wear, adding a pom-pom at the tip and scallop trim around the opening makes each hat personalized for a guest. As a bonus, fill large cellophane bags with popcorn, shaping into cones to fit the hats. Insert a bag into each hat to keep guests both fed and festive.

Simply Stitched

MITTEN SMITTEN

This cute trim is so light it won't weigh down the branches no matter what type of tree you have. Use the patterns on page 157 to cut a small mitten from a colored scouring cloth or felt and the larger mitten from white. Cut stripes and polka dots from contrasting colors of scouring cloth or felt. Use a needle threaded with white embroidery floss to add simple running stitches to hold motifs in place and to add details and definition to the shape. Cut a ½×5-inch length of blue for the hanger; trim the ends into points. Cross over the ends of the strip and attach it to the upper right corner of the mitten with a cross-stitch. Center and hot-glue the stitched mitten to the white mitten.

JOLLY JAR WRAP

Dress a plain jar for the holidays with a sleeve that takes just minutes to orchestrate. Cut a piece from a red scouring cloth or felt to encase the jar. Cut a wide stripe of pink to accent the base piece; stitch the shapes together using white embroidery floss and running stitches. Using the pattern on page 157, cut a green holly leaf and outline it with running stitches. Arrange the leaf on the band as shown and stitch it down the center, attaching it to the base. Use cross-stitches to attach a trio of ¾-inch red and pink holly berries. Add running stitches along the long ends and just below the stripe. Accent the base with cross-stitches, just to the left of the holly. With short ends together, stitch the seam closed. Slip the jar into the sleeve.

STAR-STUDDED CARD CADDY

Add a personal touch to giving gift cards—present them in handmade holders that can showcase any simple motif on the front. Cut a 3½×4½-inch rectangle from a blue scouring cloth or felt and a yellow 3½×5-inch piece for the back. Use the pattern on page 157 to cut a star shape from yellow. Cut two pink circles for cheeks. With white embroidery floss, stitch the cheeks to the star using cross-stitches. Stitch the eyes, nose, and smile. Place the star at an angle and stitch to the cardholder front with long stitches around the edge. Aligning the bottom short edges of the holder front and back, stitch the sides and bottoms together with running stitches, leaving a narrow border. Stitch cross-stitches at the top, flanking the opening.

SHARE-A-SMILE GIFT TAG

This happy guy is so cheerful, he can go straight from the gift bag to a special spot on the tree. Cut a 2½-inch circle from a white scouring cloth or felt. Cut a 1×2-inch hat and a ¼×3-inch brim piece from blue. Slip the hat piece slightly under the brim piece. Using white embroidery floss, stitch the pieces together along the brim and outline the hat, attaching the head piece as the bottom of the brim is stitched. Attach a ⅜-inch pink circle nose to the center of the face using a cross-stitch. Cut a ½×5-inch strip from yellow, trimming the ends into points; outline the shape with white running stitches. Tie a knot in the center and attach to the snowman at the lower left edge of the face. Use black floss and running stitches to make the eyes and smile. Poke the end of a white chenille stem through the hat top, twisting the ends together to hang the snowman.

A-TREE-TO-BEHOLD GREETING CARD

No extra postage needed for this light-as-a-feather greeting. Use the pattern on page 157 to cut the tree shape from a green scouring cloth or felt. Use white embroidery floss and running stitches to outline the shape and add yellow garlands. For the ornaments, cut small circles of various-color cloth or felt; attach using cross-stitches. Use hot glue to attach the tree to a 4½×6½-inch piece of white cardstock. Use double-sided tape to attach the white cardstock to a 5×7-inch piece of red cardstock.

food

Spread the joy of the season with recipes that will become holiday favorites for years to come.

BOURBON TOFFEE COOKIES AND BOURBON BALL
Recipes on page 103

WINTER SLAW WITH
BLOOD ORANGE
VINAIGRETTE
Recipe on page 115

Rise & Dine

Build a company-worthy breakfast or brunch with these savory and sweet recipes that come to the table in one dish.

**CHEESY POTATO BAKE
WITH EGGS**
Recipe on page 90

BISCUITS AND GRAVY BREAKFAST CASSEROLE
Recipe on page 90

Food

BISCUITS AND GRAVY BREAKFAST CASSEROLE

Photo on page 89

HANDS-ON TIME 15 minutes
CHILL 2 hours
BAKE 9 minutes at 400°F + 50 minutes at 350°F
STAND 10 minutes

WHAT YOU NEED
- 2 12-oz. tubes refrigerated flaky biscuits (20 biscuits total)
- 1 lb. bulk pork sausage, browned and drained
- 1 cup shredded white cheddar cheese (4 oz.)
- 8 eggs
- 4 cups milk
- ¼ tsp. black pepper
- 2 Tbsp. butter
- 1 Tbsp. all-purpose flour

WHAT YOU DO
1. Preheat oven to 400°F. Quarter biscuits. Spread biscuits in a single layer on two large baking sheets. Bake 9 to 11 minutes or until golden. Cool on baking sheets on a wire rack.

2. Grease a 3-qt. rectangular baking dish. Place half the biscuit pieces in the prepared dish. Top with 1½ cups sausage and half of the cheese (cover and chill remaining sausage until needed). Top with remaining biscuits.

3. In a large bowl whisk together eggs, 3 cups of the milk, and ⅛ tsp. of the pepper. Pour egg mixture over biscuits in dish. Using the back of a spoon, gently press down on layers to moisten. Top with remaining cheese. Cover and chill at least 2 hours or overnight.

4. Preheat oven to 350°F. Uncover dish. Bake 50 minutes or until puffed, golden, and set. Cover with foil the last 5 to 10 minutes of baking, if needed to prevent overbrowning. Let stand 10 minutes before serving.

5. Meanwhile, in a small saucepan melt butter over medium. Whisk in flour and remaining ⅛ tsp. pepper. Whisk in remaining 1 cup milk. Cook and stir until thickened and bubbly. Stir in remaining ½ cup sausage. Cook and stir 1 minute more. Spoon gravy over casserole before serving. Makes 12 servings.

CHEESY POTATO BAKE WITH EGGS

Photo on page 88

HANDS-ON TIME 35 minutes
BAKE 55 minutes at 325°F

WHAT YOU NEED
- 2 Tbsp. butter
- ½ cup finely chopped onion
- 4 tsp. all-purpose flour
- 1 tsp. salt
- ¾ tsp. black pepper
- 1½ cups milk
- 2 cups shredded sharp cheddar cheese (8 oz.)
- 3 lb. russet potatoes, peeled and thinly sliced
- 1 Tbsp. vegetable oil
- 1½ cups chopped fresh or frozen broccoli
- 8 eggs
- 6 slices bacon, crisp-cooked, drained, and crumbled
- 1 large tomato, chopped

WHAT YOU DO
1. Preheat oven to 325°F. For cheese sauce, in a medium saucepan melt butter over medium. Add onion; cook 4 minutes or until tender, stirring occasionally. Stir in flour, ½ tsp. of the salt, and ½ tsp. of the pepper. Stir in milk; cook and stir until slightly thickened and bubbly. Add cheese, stirring until melted.

2. In a 3-qt. rectangular baking dish layer potatoes and cheese sauce. Bake, covered, 55 minutes or until potatoes are tender.

3. In a large skillet heat oil over medium. Add broccoli; cook 5 minutes or until almost tender, stirring frequently. In a large bowl beat together eggs, 2 Tbsp. water, and the remaining ½ tsp. salt and ¼ tsp. pepper. Pour over broccoli in skillet. Cook over medium, without stirring, until mixture begins to set on the bottom and around the edges. Using a spatula, lift and fold partially cooked egg mixture so the uncooked portion flows underneath. Continue cooking 2 minutes more or until egg mixture is cooked but still glossy and moist. Spoon eggs over potatoes. Top with bacon and tomato. Serve immediately. Makes 8 servings.

CHEESY CHORIZO SHEET-PAN FRITTATA

HANDS-ON TIME 15 minutes
BAKE 10 minutes at 450°F

WHAT YOU NEED
- Nonstick cooking spray
- 8 oz. uncooked chorizo or bulk pork sausage
- 1 fresh poblano pepper, seeded and chopped*
- ½ cup chopped onion
- 1 15-oz. can reduced-sodium black beans, rinsed and drained
- ½ 12-oz. jar roasted red sweet peppers, drained and chopped
- 18 eggs
- ½ tsp. salt
- ¼ tsp. black pepper
- ¾ cup shredded Mexican cheese blend or cheddar cheese (3 oz.)
- 2 Tbsp. chopped fresh cilantro
- Chopped tomato, sliced avocado, and/or fried tortilla strips (optional)

WHAT YOU DO
1. Preheat oven to 450°F. Generously coat a 15×10-inch baking pan with cooking spray.

2. In a large skillet cook sausage, poblano pepper, and onion over medium until sausage is browned; drain any fat. Stir in beans and roasted peppers. Spread into prepared pan.

3. In a large bowl whisk together eggs, salt, and black pepper. Stir in cheese and cilantro. Pour egg mixture over sausage mixture. Bake 10 to 12 minutes or until set. If using, top with tomato, avocado, and/or tortilla strips. Sprinkle with additional cheese and cilantro. Makes 12 servings.

*Tip Chile peppers contain oils that can irritate your skin and eyes. Wear plastic or rubber gloves when working with them.

CHEESY CHORIZO
SHEET-PAN FRITTATA

SPINACH-PANCETTA QUICHE

HANDS-ON TIME 1 hour
BAKE 30 minutes at 400°F + 80 minutes at 325°F
COOL 50 minutes

WHAT YOU NEED

1   recipe Deep-Dish Pastry Shell
8   oz. pancetta, chopped
2   large onions, thinly sliced
½   tsp. dried thyme, crushed
½   cup dried tomatoes in olive oil, drained and chopped
4   cups fresh baby spinach
2   cups shredded Havarti cheese (8 oz.)
6   eggs
2   cups plain fat-free Greek yogurt
1   cup milk
½   tsp. salt
¼   tsp. white pepper
⅛   tsp. ground nutmeg
    Fresh basil (optional)

WHAT YOU DO

1. Prepare Deep-Dish Pastry Shell. Preheat oven to 400°F. Line unpricked pastry with a double thickness of foil, extending foil over side. Bake 20 minutes or until edge of pastry is light brown. Remove foil. Bake 10 to 15 minutes more or until bottom is light brown. Cool on a wire rack.
2. In a 10-inch skillet cook pancetta over medium 10 to 12 minutes or until lightly browned, stirring occasionally. Using a slotted spoon, transfer pancetta to paper towels, reserving 2 Tbsp. drippings in skillet. Add onions and thyme to reserved drippings; cook over medium 20 to 22 minutes or until golden, stirring occasionally. Stir in dried tomatoes; cook 1 minute. Add spinach; cook 1 to 2 minutes or until wilted. Cool 10 minutes. Stir in cheese and pancetta.

3. Meanwhile, reduce oven to 325°F. In a blender combine eggs and next five ingredients (through nutmeg). Cover and blend until frothy. Spoon spinach mixture into pastry shell; add egg mixture. Place springform pan in a shallow baking pan.
4. Bake 80 to 90 minutes or until top is lightly browned and filling is just set in center (165°F). Cool in pan on a wire rack 40 minutes. Using a serrated knife, trim pastry flush with top of pan. Remove side of pan. If using, top quiche with basil. Makes 10 servings.

To Make Ahead Prepare and bake Deep-Dish Pastry Shell; cool. Store, covered, at room temperature overnight or place in a resealable freezer bag and freeze up to 6 months.

Deep-Dish Pastry Shell In a food processor combine 2 cups all-purpose flour and 1 tsp. salt. Add ½ cup cold unsalted butter, cut up; cover and pulse until mixture resembles coarse crumbs. Combine 1 lightly beaten egg and ¼ cup cold water; add to flour mixture. Cover and pulse just until mixture begins to come together. Shape into a disk and wrap in plastic wrap. Chill at least 30 minutes. On a lightly floured surface, roll pastry into a 15-inch circle. Transfer to a 9-inch springform pan; gently press into pan. Trim overhanging pastry to 1 inch and press firmly against outside edge. Fill any cracks with trimmings. Freeze pastry shell 20 minutes before baking.

CINNAMON TOAST BREAD-
AND-BUTTER PUDDING

CHOCOLATE-HAZELNUT SWIRL COFFEE CAKE

HANDS ON 25 minutes
BAKE 1 hour at 350°F
COOL 45 minutes

WHAT YOU NEED

1   recipe Streusel
1   8-oz. pkg. cream cheese, softened
⅓   cup chocolate-hazelnut spread
1¾   cups granulated sugar
3½   cups all-purpose flour
1½   tsp. baking powder
½   tsp. baking soda
⅔   cup butter, cut up
1½   cups buttermilk or sour milk
2   eggs, lightly beaten
2   tsp. vanilla

WHAT YOU DO

1. Preheat oven to 350°F. Grease and flour a 9-inch springform pan. Prepare Streusel.
2. For filling, in a medium bowl beat together cream cheese, chocolate-hazelnut spread, and ¼ cup of the sugar with a mixer on medium until smooth.
3. In a large bowl stir together remaining 1½ cups sugar, the flour, baking powder, and baking soda. Using a pastry blender, cut in butter until mixture resembles coarse crumbs. Make a well in the center of the flour mixture. In a bowl whisk together buttermilk, eggs, and vanilla. Add buttermilk mixture to the flour mixture. Stir just until moistened (batter should be lumpy).
4. Spread half of the batter into prepared pan. Spread filling over top and sprinkle with 1 cup of the Streusel. Drop remaining batter in small mounds onto layers in pan and spread until even; sprinkle with remaining Streusel.
5. Bake 60 to 70 minutes or until golden and a toothpick comes out clean. Cool in pan on a wire rack 15 minutes. Remove sides of pan; cool on a wire rack 30 minutes. Serve warm. Makes 12 servings.
Streusel In a medium bowl stir together 1½ cups all-purpose flour, ¾ cup packed brown sugar, ½ tsp. ground cinnamon, and ¼ tsp. salt. Add ½ cup melted butter and ½ tsp. vanilla; toss with a fork to combine. Stir in ½ cup miniature semisweet chocolate chips and ¼ cup finely chopped hazelnuts.

CINNAMON TOAST BREAD-AND-BUTTER PUDDING

HANDS-ON TIME 20 minutes
STAND 5 minutes
BAKE 35 minutes at 375°F
COOL 30 minutes

WHAT YOU NEED

6   Tbsp. salted butter, softened
¼   cup plus 1½ tsp. sugar
1½   tsp. ground cinnamon
6   slices brioche sandwich bread, sliced ½ inch thick
1½   cups half-and-half
3   large eggs
1   tsp. vanilla
⅛   tsp. fine sea salt

WHAT YOU DO

1. Preheat oven to 375°F. Butter a 2- to 2½-qt. baking dish.
2. In a small bowl stir together butter, 1 Tbsp. of the sugar, and ½ tsp. of the cinnamon until creamy; spread on bread slices. Press slices together to make three sandwiches. Cut sandwiches diagonally into quarters; arrange in prepared baking dish with corners pointing up slightly.
3. In a bowl whisk together half-and-half, eggs, 3 Tbsp. of the sugar, ¾ tsp. of the cinnamon, the vanilla, and salt. Pour mixture over bread. Using the back of a spoon, gently press down on layers to moisten; let stand 5 minutes.
4. In a small bowl stir together the remaining 1½ tsp. sugar and ¼ tsp. cinnamon. Sprinkle over top.
5. Bake 35 minutes or until puffed and golden and a knife comes out clean. Cool on a wire rack 30 minutes. Serve warm. Makes 8 servings.

CHOCOLATE-
HAZELNUT SWIRL
COFFEE CAKE

Eat, Drink & Be Merry

Looking for a fun twist for your next party? Choose from enticing combinations—these spirited cookies and cocktails are meant to be together.

LIMONCELLO CHEESECAKE BARS

HANDS-ON TIME 20 minutes
BAKE 28 minutes at 350°F
COOL 1 hour
CHILL 2 hours

WHAT YOU NEED

2   cups graham cracker crumbs
¼   cup sugar
2   tsp. lemon zest
½   cup butter, melted
2   8-oz. pkg. cream cheese, softened
⅔   cup sugar
2   tsp. vanilla
½   cup limoncello (Italian lemon liqueur)
2   eggs
1   recipe Candied Lemon Slices

WHAT YOU DO

1. Preheat oven to 350°F. Line a 13×9-inch baking pan with foil, extending foil over edges. In a medium bowl stir together graham cracker crumbs, the ¼ cup sugar, and the lemon zest. Add melted butter; stir until combined. Spread in bottom of prepared pan; press firmly. Bake 8 minutes or until lightly browned. Remove and cool on a wire rack.
2. For filling, in a large bowl beat cream cheese, the ⅔ cup sugar, and the vanilla with a mixer on medium until combined. Beat in limoncello until smooth. Beat in eggs just until combined. Pour filling over baked crust. Bake 20 minutes or until set. Cool in pan on wire rack 1 hour. Chill at least 2 hours.
3. Using foil, lift out uncut bars. Cut into bars. Top bars with Candied Lemon Slices. Refrigerate up to 3 days. Makes 32 servings.

Candied Lemon Slices Cut 2 lemons into ¼-inch-thick slices; remove seeds. Roll slices in sugar to coat (about 3 Tbsp.). Heat an extra-large skillet over medium-high. Add lemon slices in a single layer. Cook 3 to 4 minutes per side or until glazed and starting to brown. Remove; cool on a piece of foil or parchment paper. Roll in additional sugar to coat. Cut each slice into quarters.

LIMONCELLO SPARKLER

START TO FINISH 10 minutes

WHAT YOU NEED

6   Tbsp. (3 oz.) Prosecco or other sparkling wine, chilled
2   Tbsp. (1 oz.) fresh tangerine juice
1   Tbsp. (½ oz.) limoncello (Italian lemon liqueur)
    Ice cubes
    Tangerine peel twist

WHAT YOU DO

1. In a cocktail glass combine Prosecco, tangerine juice, and limoncello. Add ice and garnish with a twist of tangerine peel. Makes 1 serving.

RUMCHATA SNICKERDOODLES

Photo on page 98

HANDS-ON TIME 30 minutes
CHILL 1 hour
BAKE 8 minutes per batch at 375°F

WHAT YOU NEED

1   cup butter, softened
1¾   cups sugar
1   tsp. baking soda
1   tsp. cream of tartar
¼   tsp. salt
2   eggs
¼   cup RumChata liqueur
½   tsp. vanilla
3   cups all-purpose flour
2   tsp. ground cinnamon

WHAT YOU DO

1. In a large bowl beat butter with a mixer on medium to high 30 seconds. Add 1½ cups of the sugar, the baking soda, cream of tartar, and salt. Beat until combined, scraping bowl as needed. Beat in eggs, RumChata, and vanilla until combined. Beat in as much flour as you can with the mixer. Stir in any remaining flour. Cover and chill 1 hour or until dough is easy to handle.
2. Preheat oven to 375°F. In a small bowl combine the remaining ¼ cup sugar and the cinnamon. Shape dough into 1¼-inch balls. Roll balls in sugar mixture to coat. Place 2 inches apart on ungreased cookie sheets.
3. Bake 8 minutes or until bottoms are lightly browned. Remove and cool on wire racks. Makes 48 servings.

CINNAMON TOAST ON THE ROCKS

Photo on page 98

START TO FINISH 10 minutes

WHAT YOU NEED

    Cinnamon sugar
    Ice cubes
3   to 4 Tbsp. (1½ to 2 oz.) RumChata liqueur
3   to 4 Tbsp. (1½ to 2 oz.) cinnamon whiskey (such as Fireball)

WHAT YOU DO

1. Wet the rim of a rocks glass with water and dip in cinnamon sugar to coat; fill glass with ice. Fill a cocktail shaker halfway with ice. Add RumChata and cinnamon whiskey. Cover and shake until very cold. Strain liquid into prepared glass. Makes 1 serving.

LIMONCELLO
CHEESECAKE BARS
AND LIMONCELLO
SPARKLER

**RUMCHATA SNICKERDOODLES
AND CINNAMON TOAST ON
THE ROCKS**
Recipes on page 96

**KAHLUA CHOCOLATE
CRINKLES AND
MUDSLIDE**
Recipes on page 100

Food

KAHLUA CHOCOLATE CRINKLES

Photo on page 98

HANDS-ON TIME 20 minutes
CHILL 30 minutes
BAKE 9 minutes per batch at 350°F
COOL 2 minutes

WHAT YOU NEED

4 oz. unsweetened chocolate, chopped
½ cup shortening
¼ cup butter
3 eggs, lightly beaten
1¾ cups granulated sugar
2 tsp. baking powder
¼ tsp. baking soda
¼ tsp. salt
3 Tbsp. coffee-flavor liqueur (such as Kahlua)
1 tsp. vanilla
1⅓ cups all-purpose flour
⅓ cup unsweetened cocoa powder
2 Tbsp. instant espresso coffee powder
   Nonstick cooking spray
¼ cup granulated sugar
⅔ cup powdered sugar

WHAT YOU DO

1. In a 1-qt. saucepan heat and stir chocolate, shortening, and butter over low until melted. Cool.
2. In a bowl combine the next five ingredients (through salt). Stir in melted chocolate mixture, the liqueur, and vanilla. Stir in flour, cocoa powder, and espresso powder. Cover and chill at least 30 minutes or until dough is easy to handle.
3. Preheat oven to 350°F. Coat cookie sheets with cooking spray. Shape dough into 1½-inch balls. Roll balls in the ¼ cup granulated sugar then in powdered sugar to coat. Place balls 2 inches apart on prepared cookie sheets. Bake 9 to 11 minutes or just until edges are firm and cracks appear slightly moist. Cool on cookie sheets 2 minutes. Remove; cool on wire racks. Makes 32 servings.

MUDSLIDE

Photo on page 99

START TO FINISH 5 minutes

WHAT YOU NEED

   Chocolate-flavor syrup
   Ice cubes
1½ Tbsp. (¾ oz.) coffee-flavor liqueur (such as Kahlua)
1½ Tbsp. (¾ oz.) Irish cream liqueur
1½ Tbsp. (¾ oz.) half-and-half
1½ Tbsp. (¾ oz.) vodka (optional)

WHAT YOU DO

1. Drizzle chocolate syrup around the inside rim of a chilled cocktail glass. Fill a cocktail shaker halfway with ice. Add liqueurs, half-and-half, and vodka (if using). Cover and shake until very cold. Strain liquid into prepared glass. If desired, add ice. Makes 1 serving.

EARL GREY HOT BUTTERED RUM

START TO FINISH 10 minutes

WHAT YOU NEED

½ cup boiling water
2 tsp. packed brown sugar
1 Earl Grey tea bag
2 Tbsp. (1 oz.) dark rum
1½ tsp. Spiced Butter

WHAT YOU DO

1. In a mug stir together boiling water and brown sugar until sugar dissolves. Add tea bag; steep 5 minutes. Remove and discard tea bag. Add rum. Top with Spiced Butter. Makes 1 serving.
Spiced Butter In a small bowl combine ½ cup softened butter and 1 tsp. pumpkin pie spice. Roll into a log and wrap in plastic wrap. Chill until firm.

FRUITCAKE BARS

HAND-ON TIME 30 minutes
BAKE 45 minutes at 350°F

WHAT YOU NEED

4 cups packed brown sugar
1⅓ cups butter
4 cups all-purpose flour
2 tsp. baking powder
1 tsp. ground cinnamon
½ tsp. baking soda
4 eggs
¾ cup rum or brandy
1 Tbsp. vanilla
3 cups coarsely chopped pecans
1 cup candied cherries, chopped
1 cup golden raisins, chopped
½ cup candied pineapple, chopped

WHAT YOU DO

1. Preheat oven to 350°F. In a 4- to 5-qt. pot cook and stir brown sugar and butter over medium until melted and smooth. Cool 10 minutes.
2. Meanwhile, line a 13×9-inch baking pan with foil, extending foil over edges. Grease foil. In a medium bowl stir together flour, baking powder, cinnamon, and baking soda. Stir eggs, rum, and vanilla into brown sugar mixture. Stir in flour mixture. Fold in remaining ingredients until combined. Spread in prepared baking pan.
3. Bake 45 minutes or until evenly browned and set. Cool in pan on a wire rack. Using foil, lift out uncut bars. Cut into bars. Refrigerate up to 3 days. Makes 36 servings.

FRUITCAKE BARS
AND EARL GREY HOT
BUTTERED RUM

MARGARITA
SHORTBREAD
SLICES AND
EL DIABLO

MARGARITA SHORTBREAD SLICES

HANDS-ON TIME 20 minutes
CHILL 3 hours
BAKE 12 minutes per batch at 325°F

WHAT YOU NEED
¾ cup butter, softened
⅓ cup powdered sugar
1 Tbsp. lime zest
3 Tbsp. tequila
1 tsp. vanilla
1¾ cups all-purpose flour
2 Tbsp. cornstarch
¾ tsp. salt
Coarse white decorating sugar
1 recipe Tequila Icing

WHAT YOU DO
1. In a large bowl beat butter with a mixer on medium 30 seconds. Add powdered sugar, lime zest, tequila, and vanilla. Beat until combined, scraping bowl as needed. Beat in flour, cornstarch, and salt.
2. Divide dough in half. Shape each portion into a 10-inch roll. Coat each roll with coarse sugar. If desired, sprinkle rolls with additional lime zest. Wrap rolls in plastic wrap or waxed paper. Chill 3 hours or until firm enough to slice.
3. Preheat oven to 325°F. Line cookie sheets with parchment paper. Using a sharp, thin-bladed knife, cut rolls into ¼-inch slices. Place 2 inches apart on prepared cookie sheets. Bake 12 to 15 minutes or just until bottoms are golden. Transfer cookies on parchment to wire racks to cool. Drizzle cooled cookies with Tequila Icing. If desired, sprinkle with additional lime zest. Makes 36 servings.
Tequila Icing In a medium bowl combine 1 cup powdered sugar, 1 Tbsp. tequila, and 1 Tbsp. milk. Whisk until smooth, adding more milk, 1 tsp. at a time, to reach spreading consistency.

EL DIABLO

START TO FINISH 5 minutes

WHAT YOU NEED
Ice cubes
1½ Tbsp. (¾ oz.) silver tequila
1 Tbsp. (½ oz.) lime juice
1½ tsp. (¼ oz.) créme de cassis
3 Tbsp. (1½ oz.) ginger beer
Lime wedge and/or fresh blackberry

BOURBON TOFFEE COOKIES AND BOURBON BALL

WHAT YOU DO
1. Fill a cocktail shaker halfway with ice. Add tequila, lime juice, and créme de cassis. Cover and shake until very cold. Strain liquid into an ice-filled rocks glass. Top with ginger beer. Garnish with a lime wedge and/or a blackberry. Makes 1 serving.

BOURBON TOFFEE COOKIES

HANDS-ON TIME 20 minutes
BAKE 7 minutes per batch at 375°F
COOL 2 minutes

WHAT YOU NEED
1 cup butter, softened
1 cup packed brown sugar
½ cup granulated sugar
1 tsp. baking soda
¾ tsp. salt
2 eggs
1 tsp. vanilla
½ cup bourbon
2¾ cups all-purpose flour
12 oz. semisweet chocolate chunks (2 cups)
½ cup almond toffee bits

WHAT YOU DO
1. Preheat oven to 375°F. In a large bowl beat butter with a mixer on medium to high 30 seconds. Add the next four ingredients (through salt). Beat on medium 2 minutes, scraping bowl as needed. Beat in eggs, vanilla, and bourbon until combined. Beat in as much of the flour as you can with the mixer. Stir in any remaining flour. Stir in chocolate and toffee pieces.
2. Drop dough by small spoonfuls 2 inches apart onto ungreased cookie sheets. Bake 7 to 9 minutes or until edges are golden brown. Cool on cookie sheets 2 minutes. Remove; cool on wire racks. Makes 60 servings.

BOURBON BALL

START TO FINISH 5 minutes

WHAT YOU NEED
Ice cubes
1½ Tbsp. (¾ oz.) bourbon
1 Tbsp. (½ oz.) créme de cacao
1½ Tbsp. (¼ oz.) hazelnut liqueur (such as Frangelico)
Chocolate shavings

WHAT YOU DO
1. Fill a cocktail shaker halfway with ice. Add bourbon, créme de cacao, and liqueur. Cover and shake until very cold. Strain liquid into a cocktail glass. Top with chocolate shavings. Makes 1 serving.

HAZELNUT MACARONS

HANDS-ON TIME 50 minutes
STAND 15 minutes
BAKE 10 minutes per batch at 325°F

WHAT YOU NEED

3   egg whites, room temperature
⅔   cup granulated sugar
⅛   tsp. kosher salt
⅛   tsp. cream of tartar
1   tsp. hazelnut liqueur (such as Frangelico)
1¾ cups powdered sugar
1   cup almond flour
¾   cup ground and sifted hazelnuts*
1   recipe Hazelnut Buttercream Filling
2   egg whites, room temperature

WHAT YOU DO

1. Line three large cookie sheets with parchment paper. On a fourth sheet of parchment paper, use a permanent marker to draw 1½-inch circles, 1 inch apart, to create a pattern. Set aside.
2. Fill a 2-qt. saucepan with 1½ inches water. Bring to boiling over medium-high. Reduce heat to medium-low to maintain a gentle simmer. For meringue, in the metal bowl of a stand mixer combine the 3 egg whites, the granulated sugar, salt, and cream of tartar. Place bowl over simmering water, making sure water does not touch bottom of bowl. Cook 8 to 10 minutes or until sugar is dissolved (about 150°F), stirring constantly with a rubber or silicone spatula.
3. Return bowl to stand mixer. Using the whisk attachment, beat egg white mixture on high 8 to 10 minutes or until stiff peaks form (tips stand straight) and bowl is cool to the touch. Add hazelnut liqueur the last 1 minute of beating.
4. Meanwhile, using a coarse-mesh sieve, sift together powdered sugar, almond flour, and ground hazelnuts into a large

bowl. Discard any larger pieces (up to 1 Tbsp. total) that remain in sieve. Add the 2 egg whites to flour mixture; stir with a spatula until a thick paste forms. The mixture may seem crumbly at first but will come together after mixing.
5. Fold and press one-third of the meringue into almond-hazelnut paste. Repeat, folding and pressing in remaining meringue by thirds. Batter will be thick at first but will loosen as you fold. Pressing the mixture during folding helps to release air bubbles. Continue folding until batter falls off the spatula in a thick ribbon and you can draw a figure 8. Batter should be loose enough that it does not hold its shape but stiff enough that you can still see the figure 8 after 10 seconds. (It is better to slightly undermix than to overmix.)
6. Fit a pastry bag with a ¼-inch round tip. Fill bag two-thirds full with batter.
7. For each batch, slide parchment pattern under the plain parchment sheet on a cookie sheet. Pipe batter onto parchment, stopping just before batter reaches the outline of circle. Firmly tap cookie sheet five to 10 times on the counter to release air bubbles. Using a toothpick or the tip of a sharp knife, pop any remaining bubbles that come to the surface. Slide out parchment pattern; repeat with remaining prepared cookie sheets. Let stand 15 minutes or until tops are dry to the touch.
8. Meanwhile, preheat oven to 325°F. Bake macarons, one sheet at a time, 10 to 12 minutes. Tops of cookies should be firm and not slide when gently touched. Immediately slide parchment paper off cookie sheet onto the counter; allow macarons to cool completely.
9. Prepare Hazelnut Buttercream Filling. Spread filling onto bottoms of half of the macarons, using about 1½ tsp. for each. Top with remaining macarons, bottom

sides down. Refrigerate up to 5 days or freeze up to 2 months. Makes 45 servings.
*Tip For ground hazelnuts, place 6 oz. hazelnuts in a food processor. Pulse to make a fine powder. Sift ground hazelnuts through a coarse-mesh sieve and measure ¾ cup.
Hazelnut Buttercream Filling In an extra-large bowl beat ½ cup softened butter with a mixer on medium 1 to 2 minutes or until creamy. Beat in ½ cup powdered sugar. Beat in 1 Tbsp. heavy cream and dash salt on low until combined. Gradually beat in 1½ cups additional powdered sugar just until combined. Beat on medium 5 minutes or until light and fluffy, scraping bowl as needed. Beat in 2 Tbsp. hazelnut liqueur on high 1 minute more. If desired, beat in 2 Tbsp. chocolate hazelnut spread.

NUTS AND BERRIES

START TO FINISH 5 minutes

WHAT YOU NEED
   Ice cubes
1½ Tbsp. (¾ oz.) hazelnut liqueur (such as Frangelico)
1½ Tbsp. (¾ oz.) black raspberry liqueur (such as Chambord)
1½ Tbsp. (¾ oz.) half-and-half
   Fresh raspberries (optional)
   Freshly grated nutmeg

WHAT YOU DO

1. Fill a rocks glass with ice. Add liqueurs. Drizzle with half-and-half. If desired, top with a fresh raspberry and a light grating of nutmeg. Makes 1 serving.

In-Season Soups

Cool weather invites warm-up recipes, like these hearty stews of seasonal vegetables, toothsome grains, and comforting flavor combinations. All are easy to tailor to your family's liking.

CARIBBEAN TURKEY AND SWEET POTATO SOUP
Recipe on page 109

CHIPOTLE CHICKEN-
SQUASH CHILI
Recipe on page 109

SPICY SAUSAGE
AND COLLARD
SOUP

SPICY SAUSAGE AND COLLARD SOUP

HANDS-ON TIME 25 minutes
COOK 30 minutes

WHAT YOU NEED

- 1   lb. spicy bulk Italian sausage
- 1   onion, chopped
- 1   red bell pepper, seeded and chopped
- 2   cloves garlic, minced
- 1   32-oz. carton reduced-sodium chicken broth
- 1   15-oz. can cannellini beans, rinsed and drained
- 1   14.5-oz. can diced tomatoes, undrained
- 1   4×1-inch Parmesan rind (optional)
- 1   bay leaf
- 1   tsp. Italian seasoning, crushed
- 1   8-oz. bunch collard greens or kale, stemmed and chopped* (5 cups)
- ½   cup chopped fresh basil
     Grated Parmesan cheese

WHAT YOU DO

1. In a 5-qt. Dutch oven cook the first four ingredients (through garlic) over medium until sausage is browned, breaking into small pieces as it cooks. Add broth, beans, tomatoes, Parmesan rind (if using), bay leaf, and Italian seasoning. Bring to boiling. Reduce heat and simmer, covered, 20 minutes, stirring occasionally.
2. Remove bay leaf and Parmesan rind, if using. Add collard greens. Return to boiling. Reduce heat and simmer, covered, 10 minutes or until collards are tender. Remove from heat and stir in basil. Top servings with additional basil and Parmesan cheese. Makes 6 servings.
*Tip To prepare the collard greens, remove the inner stem of each collard leaf by cutting along each side of the stem with a sharp knife. Remove and discard the stem (or save for another use). Chop the leaves into bite-size pieces.

CARIBBEAN TURKEY AND SWEET POTATO SOUP

Photo on page 106

HANDS-ON TIME 15 minutes
SLOW COOK 4 hours 30 minutes on low

WHAT YOU NEED

     Nonstick cooking spray
- 1½ lb. boneless turkey breast, cut into 1-inch pieces
- ½   cup chopped onion
- 2   Tbsp. finely chopped fresh ginger
- 1   tsp. ground allspice
- 1   tsp. ground cumin
- ¾   tsp. black pepper
- ½   tsp. salt
- ½   tsp. garlic salt
- ½   tsp. dried thyme, crushed
- 2   large sweet potatoes, peeled and cut into 2-inch pieces
- 2   cups reduced-sodium chicken broth
- 1   14-oz. can unsweetened light coconut milk
- 2   cups cooked white rice*
- 1   15-oz. can black beans, rinsed and drained
- 3   Tbsp. snipped fresh cilantro
- 2   Tbsp. lime juice

WHAT YOU DO

1. Lightly coat a 4- to 5-qt. slow cooker with cooking spray. Place turkey in prepared cooker.
2. In a small bowl combine onion, ginger, allspice, cumin, ½ tsp. of the pepper, ¼ tsp. of the salt, the garlic salt, and thyme. Pour over turkey; stir to coat. Add sweet potatoes, broth, and coconut milk.
3. Cover and cook on low 4½ hours, stirring in rice, beans, and remaining ¼ tsp. each of the salt and pepper the last 10 minutes of cooking.
4. Stir in cilantro and lime juice. Makes 8 servings.
*Tip To make the rice, combine 1 cup long grain rice and 2 cups water in a saucepan. Bring to boiling; reduce heat to low and simmer, covered, 15 minutes. Remove from heat and let stand 5 minutes before using.

CHIPOTLE CHICKEN-SQUASH CHILI

Photo on page 107

HANDS-ON TIME 20 minutes
COOK 45 minutes

WHAT YOU NEED

- ¼   cup olive oil
- 1   medium onion, chopped
- 1   medium green bell pepper, seeded and chopped
- 1   medium poblano pepper, seeded and chopped
- 1   small butternut squash, peeled, seeded, and cut into ½- to ¾-inch pieces (3½ cups)
- 2   cloves garlic, minced
- 2   Tbsp. chili powder
- 2   Tbsp. tomato paste
- 3   cups shredded rotisserie chicken
- 2   14.5-oz. cans reduced-sodium chicken broth
- 1   15-oz. can black beans, rinsed and drained
- 1   14.5-oz. can diced fire-roasted tomatoes, undrained
- 1   canned chipotle pepper, minced
     Salt and black pepper
- ½   cup chopped fresh cilantro
     Tortilla chips, shredded cheese, and/or sour cream

WHAT YOU DO

1. In a 5- to 6-qt. Dutch oven heat olive oil over medium-high. Add onion, bell pepper, and poblano pepper. Cook, stirring occasionally, 5 minutes or until onion is softened.
2. Stir in squash and garlic. Cook, stirring frequently, 5 minutes.
3. Add chili powder and tomato paste. Cook and stir 1 minute.
4. Add chicken, broth, beans, tomatoes, and chipotle pepper. Bring to boiling. Reduce heat and simmer, covered, 30 minutes.
5. Season to taste with salt and black pepper. Remove pot from heat and stir in cilantro. Top servings with tortilla chips, shredded cheese, and/or sour cream. Makes 8 servings.

CREAMY WILD RICE-MUSHROOM SOUP

HANDS-ON TIME 25 minutes
COOK 40 minutes

WHAT YOU NEED
- 2 Tbsp. butter
- 1 cup chopped onion
- ¾ cup chopped carrots
- ½ cup chopped celery
- 16 oz. fresh cremini and/or button mushrooms, sliced
- 3 cloves garlic, minced
- ½ cup dry white wine
- 6 cups vegetable broth
- ½ tsp. salt
- ¼ tsp. black pepper
- 1 cup heavy cream
- ⅓ cup all-purpose flour
- 1 recipe Cooked Wild Rice*
- 2 tsp. chopped fresh thyme

WHAT YOU DO
1. In a 5- to 6-qt. Dutch oven melt butter over medium. Add onion, carrots, and celery; cook 5 minutes or until softened, stirring occasionally. Add mushrooms and garlic; cook 10 to 15 minutes or until vegetables are tender and most of the mushroom liquid is evaporated, stirring frequently. Carefully add wine; cook and stir 1 minute more.
2. Add broth, salt, and pepper to mushroom mixture. Bring to boiling; reduce heat. Simmer 10 minutes. In a small bowl combine cream and flour; stir into broth mixture. Cook and stir until slightly thickened and bubbly. Stir in Cooked Wild Rice and thyme. Return to boiling; reduce heat. Simmer 5 minutes to blend flavors.
3. Season soup to taste with additional salt and pepper. If desired, top servings with additional thyme. Makes 8 servings.
*Tip Or use two 8.8-oz. pouches cooked long grain and wild rice.
Cooked Wild Rice In a medium saucepan combine 1½ cups water; ¾ cup wild rice, rinsed and drained; and ¼ tsp. salt. Bring to boiling; reduce heat. Simmer, covered, 40 minutes or until tender. Drain if needed.

CARROT SOUP WITH TARRAGON AND CREAM

SMOKY CAULIFLOWER-CHEESE SOUP

CARROT SOUP WITH TARRAGON AND CREAM

HANDS-ON TIME 35 minutes
COOK 22 minutes

WHAT YOU NEED
3 Tbsp. unsalted butter
2 cups peeled and thinly sliced carrots
1 cup thinly sliced leek (white and light green parts only)
½ cup chopped russet potato
1 large shallot, finely chopped
   Pinch kosher salt
1 clove garlic, finely chopped
1½ tsp. finely chopped fresh tarragon
2 Tbsp. dry white wine
1 32-oz. carton chicken broth
¼ tsp. kosher salt
¼ tsp. freshly ground black pepper
1 Tbsp. heavy cream

WHAT YOU DO
1. In a 4-qt. saucepan melt butter over medium. Add carrots, leek, potato, shallot, and the pinch salt. Cook, stirring occasionally, 10 minutes or until vegetables are softened.
2. Stir in garlic and tarragon; cook 1 minute or until fragrant. Add wine;

cook and stir 2 minutes or until nearly evaporated. Add broth; bring to boiling. Reduce heat and simmer, covered, 10 minutes or until carrots and potato are tender.
3. Cool soup slightly. Puree using an immersion blender, or transfer soup to a blender and puree in batches (return soup to saucepan) Add the ¼ tsp. salt, the pepper, and cream. Top with additional fresh tarragon. Makes 8 servings.

SMOKY CAULIFLOWER-CHEESE SOUP

HANDS-ON TIME 20 minutes
COOK 30 minutes

WHAT YOU NEED
6 slices peppered bacon
3 Tbsp. butter
½ cup finely chopped onion
1 medium head cauliflower, cut into small florets (6 cups)
1 tsp. Cajun seasoning
1 32-oz. carton reduced-sodium chicken broth
1 cup heavy cream
3 Tbsp. all-purpose flour
2 cups shredded Monterey Jack cheese (8 oz.)
1 cup shredded smoked cheddar cheese (4 oz.)
¼ cup chopped fresh flat-leaf parsley
   Salt and black pepper

WHAT YOU DO
1. In a 5- to 6-qt. Dutch oven cook bacon over medium until crisp. Drain bacon on paper towels. Crumble bacon; set aside.
2. Add butter and onion to pot. Cook over medium-high, stirring occasionally, 5 minutes or until tender and lightly golden. Add cauliflower and Cajun seasoning; cook, stirring occasionally, 5 minutes or until cauliflower starts to brown.
3. Add broth. Bring to boiling. Reduce heat and simmer, covered, 10 minutes or until cauliflower is tender.
4. In a small bowl whisk together cream and flour; add to cauliflower mixture. Cook and stir 5 minutes or until thickened and bubbly.
5. Remove from heat and gradually add cheeses, stirring until cheese is melted. Stir in parsley. Use a potato masher to mash cauliflower as desired. Stir in bacon. Season to taste with salt and pepper. If desired, top bowls with additional cheese and Cajun seasoning. Makes 6 servings.

Modern Holiday Potluck

The holidays bring invitations to gatherings of family and friends alike. Dial up your offering with this contemporary collection of inspired recipes.

BRAISED BEEF SHANKS WITH MUSHROOMS AND OLIVES

BRAISED BEEF SHANKS WITH MUSHROOMS AND OLIVES

HANDS-ON TIME 35 minutes
ROAST 2 hours at 325°F

WHAT YOU NEED
2 Tbsp. olive oil
4 lb. beef shank crosscuts, cut 1¼ inches thick

Salt and black pepper
2 cups chopped onions
1 cup coarsely chopped carrots
3 cloves garlic, minced
¾ cup dry red wine or beef broth
1 14.5-oz. can diced tomatoes with basil, garlic, and oregano, undrained
1 cup beef broth
12 oz. fresh cremini or button mushrooms, quartered or halved

¾ cup assorted pitted olives, halved
    Hot cooked gnocchi (optional)
1 recipe Gremolata

WHAT YOU DO
1. Preheat oven to 325°F. In a Dutch oven heat oil over medium-high. Add beef shanks; cook until browned on all sides. Remove shanks; sprinkle with salt and pepper.

2. Add onions, carrots, and garlic to Dutch oven. Cook 5 minutes or until tender, stirring occasionally. Carefully add wine, stirring to scrape up any crusty browned bits. Add tomatoes and broth; return beef shanks to Dutch oven. Bring to boiling. Cover pot and transfer to oven.

3. Roast 2 to 3 hours or until shanks are tender, adding mushrooms the last 20 minutes of roasting. Transfer shanks to a platter.

4. Strain vegetables from cooking liquid. Stir olives into vegetables and spoon over beef shanks. Skim fat from cooking liquid. Drizzle liquid over shanks, vegetables, and, if using, gnocchi. Sprinkle with Gremolata. Makes 8 servings.

Gremolata In a small bowl combine ¼ cup snipped fresh flat-leaf parsley, 2 tsp. lemon zest, and 3 cloves garlic, minced. Makes ¼ cup.

VEGETARIAN LASAGNA

Photo on page 114

HANDS-ON TIME 45 minutes
BAKE 45 minutes at 375°F
STAND 20 minutes

WHAT YOU NEED

3   large bunches Swiss chard, rinsed and drained (1½ to 2 lb. total)
3   cloves garlic, minced
    Olive oil
1   tsp. kosher salt
¼   tsp. ground nutmeg
12 dried lasagna noodles*
12 oz. goat cheese, room temperature
½   cup milk
1   egg
2   Tbsp. chopped fresh chives
4   cups cherry tomatoes, halved
1   cup coarsely chopped walnuts
¼   cup grated Parmesan cheese

WHAT YOU DO

1. Preheat oven to 375°F. Remove and discard thick stems from Swiss chard; coarsely chop leaves. In a large Dutch oven cook garlic in 1 Tbsp. hot oil over medium 30 seconds. Add Swiss chard in batches. Cook 2 minutes or until all the chard is slightly wilted. Sprinkle with ½ tsp. of the salt and the nutmeg.

2. Cook noodles according to package directions until tender but still firm (al dente). Drain; rinse with cold water. Drain well.

3. For filling, in a bowl whisk together goat cheese, milk, egg, chives, and the remaining ½ tsp. salt until well-combined.

4. Drizzle the bottom of a 3-qt. rectangular baking dish with additional olive oil. Arrange 3 noodles in a single layer on oil. Layer with one-fourth of the filling, one-fourth of the Swiss chard mixture, one-fourth of the cherry tomatoes, and one-fourth of the walnuts. Repeat layers three more times. Sprinkle top with Parmesan cheese. Cover with a piece of parchment paper brushed with olive oil, coated side down; seal tightly with foil.

5. Bake 30 minutes. Uncover; bake 15 minutes more or until cheese is golden and mixture is bubbly. Let stand 20 minutes. Makes 8 servings.

*Tip Because this lasagna has a thick sauce, we don't recommend using no-boil noodles.

To Make Ahead Prepare as directed through Step 1. Store wilted Swiss chard in the refrigerator up to 3 days.

GARLIC AND HERB SWIRL BREAD

Recipe on page 114

HANDS-ON TIME 30 minutes
STAND 10 minutes
RISE 1 hour 45 minutes
BAKE 30 minutes at 375°F

WHAT YOU NEED

3½ to 4 cups all-purpose flour
1   pkg. active dry yeast (2¼ tsp.)
¾   cup milk
6   Tbsp. butter, softened
2   Tbsp. sugar
1   tsp. kosher salt
3   eggs, lightly beaten
½   cup finely chopped fresh basil
¼   cup grated Parmesan cheese
2   Tbsp. finely chopped dried tomatoes (oil-packed), patted dry
1½ Tbsp. chopped fresh thyme
1   Tbsp. finely chopped fresh oregano
3   cloves garlic, minced
¼   tsp. crushed red pepper
    Melted butter (optional)

WHAT YOU DO

1. In a large bowl stir together 2 cups of the flour and the yeast. In a small saucepan heat and stir milk, 2 Tbsp. of the butter, the sugar, and salt until warm (120°F to 130°F). Stir milk mixture and eggs into flour mixture. Stir in as much of the remaining flour as you can.

2. Turn dough out onto a lightly floured surface. Knead in enough of the remaining flour to make a soft dough that is smooth, lightly tacky, and elastic (about 3 minutes). Shape dough into a ball. Place in a lightly greased bowl, turning to grease surface of dough. Cover and let rise in a warm place until nearly double in size (about 1 hour).

3. Meanwhile, in a small bowl combine the remaining 4 Tbsp. butter and the next seven ingredients (through crushed red pepper).

4. Line a baking sheet with parchment paper. Punch dough down. Turn out onto a lightly floured surface. Cover and let rest 10 minutes. Roll dough into an 18×12-inch rectangle. Spread herb butter over dough, leaving a 1-inch border on one of the long sides. Roll up rectangle, starting from the filled long side, and seal seam with fingertips. Using a serrated knife, cut roll in half lengthwise, leaving one end slightly attached. Turn dough strips cut sides up and carefully twist over each other. Pinch ends together.

5. Begin to coil the rope like a snake, stopping when you reach halfway. Coil the other half of the rope in the opposite direction to create a tight S shape. Transfer loaf to prepared baking sheet. Lightly cover with greased plastic wrap and let rise in a warm place until nearly double in size (about 45 minutes).

6. Preheat oven to 375°F. Bake 30 minutes or until golden brown and a thermometer inserted into bread registers 200°F. Brush warm bread with melted butter (if using). Sprinkle with additional chopped fresh herbs. Serve with additional butter. Makes 12 servings.

VEGETARIAN
LASAGNA
Recipe on page 113

GARLIC AND
HERB SWIRL
BREAD
*Recipe on
page 113*

AUTUMN POTATO
GRATIN

CORN CASSEROLE

CORN CASSEROLE

HANDS-ON TIME 25 minutes
BAKE 50 minutes at 350°F

WHAT YOU NEED

8	slices bacon, chopped
1½	cups chopped onions
4	cloves garlic, minced
¼	cup all-purpose flour
½	tsp. salt
¼	tsp. black pepper
2½	cups half-and-half or whole milk
2	16-oz. pkg. frozen whole kernel corn
1	14.75-oz. can cream-style corn
2	Tbsp. chopped fresh thyme leaves or 2 tsp. dried thyme, crushed
⅓	cup chopped fresh flat-leaf parsley (optional)
1	sleeve saltine crackers (40 crackers)
3	eggs, lightly beaten
¼	cup butter, melted
	Paprika (optional)

WHAT YOU DO

1. Preheat oven to 350°F. In a 4- to 5-qt. pot cook and stir bacon over medium until crisp; drain bacon on paper towels, reserving drippings. Set aside ¼ cup bacon for topping. Add onions and garlic to pot; cook and stir 2 to 3 minutes or until softened. Stir in flour, salt, and pepper. Whisk in half-and-half. Cook and stir over medium until thickened and bubbly. Stir in frozen corn, cream-style corn, thyme, the remaining bacon, and, if using, parsley.
2. Finely crush half of the crackers. Stir into corn mixture along with eggs. Spoon into a 3-qt. rectangular baking dish; cover with foil. Bake 15 minutes.
3. Meanwhile, in a medium bowl coarsely crush remaining crackers; add melted butter and toss to coat.
4. Uncover and top corn mixture with buttered crackers. If using, sprinkle with paprika. Bake, uncovered, 35 to 40 minutes more or until heated through. Sprinkle with the reserved ¼ cup bacon the last 5 minutes of baking. If using, sprinkle with additional chopped parsley. Makes 12 servings.
Add-Ins If desired, add any of the following ingredients with the corn: ½ cup drained, chopped roasted red peppers; one 4-oz. can green chile peppers, drained; 4 oz. bulk sausage, cooked and crumbled; or swap 1 cup of the corn for 1 cup frozen shelled edamame or lima beans.
Cheesy Variation Stir in 1 cup shredded cheddar cheese with the corn. Top with ½ cup shredded cheddar cheese with the bacon the last 5 minutes of baking.

AUTUMN POTATO GRATIN

HANDS-ON TIME 25 minutes
BAKE 1 hour 50 minutes at 350°F
STAND 15 minutes

WHAT YOU NEED

1½	lb. Yukon gold or other yellow-flesh potatoes, thinly sliced (about 5 cups)
1	1½-lb. butternut squash, peeled, halved, seeded, and thinly sliced crosswise
½	cup thinly sliced leek or green onions
1	Tbsp. chopped fresh sage
4	cloves garlic, minced
1	tsp. salt
½	tsp. ground nutmeg
¼	tsp. black pepper
2	cups shredded Fontina cheese (8 oz.)
1½	cups heavy cream
	Fresh sage leaves (optional)

WHAT YOU DO

1. Preheat oven to 350°F. Grease a 3-qt. rectangular baking dish. Layer half of the potatoes, half of the butternut squash, and half of the leeks in the prepared dish. Sprinkle with half of the sage, garlic, salt, nutmeg, and pepper. Sprinkle with half of the cheese. Repeat layers. Pour cream over top. Cover tightly with foil.
2. Bake, covered, 1 hour 20 minutes. Uncover; bake 30 minutes more or until potatoes are tender when pierced with a fork and top is golden brown. If using, garnish with fresh sage leaves. Let stand 15 minutes before serving. Makes 10 servings.
To Make Ahead Slice potatoes, butternut squash, and leeks. Place potatoes in a bowl of water to cover; cover with plastic wrap. Place squash and leeks in separate airtight containers; cover. Chill up to 24 hours. Drain potatoes well.

WINTER SLAW WITH BLOOD ORANGE VINAIGRETTE

Photo on page 87

START TO FINISH 25 minutes

WHAT YOU NEED

6	cups shredded stemmed kale
1	Tbsp. olive oil
1¼	tsp. kosher salt
3	cups shredded radicchio
1	cup shredded purple cabbage
⅓	cup blood orange juice
1	Tbsp. white wine vinegar
1	Tbsp. Dijon mustard
1	tsp. sugar
1	clove garlic, minced
⅓	cup olive oil
¼	tsp. black pepper
2	blood oranges, peeled and sliced
½	cup pomegranate seeds
½	cup chopped fresh flat-leaf parsley
½	cup pepitas (pumpkin seeds), toasted

WHAT YOU DO

1. In an extra-large bowl combine kale, the oil, and 1 tsp. of the salt. Using your hands, massage kale to soften the leaves. Rinse in a colander under running water; drain well and return to bowl. Add radicchio and cabbage; toss.
2. For dressing, in a small bowl whisk together the next seven ingredients (through pepper) and the remaining ¼ tsp. salt.
3. Add half of the dressing to the slaw; toss to coat. Gently stir in oranges, pomegranate seeds, and parsley. Sprinkle with pepitas. Serve salad with remaining dressing. Makes 10 servings.
To Make Ahead Prep salad and dressing as directed through Step 2. Cover; chill separately up to 48 hours.

Make-It-Mine Caramel Cracker Candy

Here it is—that sweet-salty something you've been craving. Choose from these crave-worthy options to come up with a candy all of your own.

CARAMEL CRACKER CANDY

PREP 15 minutes
BAKE 8 minutes at 350°F
STAND 5 minutes
COOL 30 minutes
CHILL 1 hour

WHAT YOU NEED
   Crackers
½ cup butter
⅓ cup packed brown sugar
½ tsp. Spice
¼ tsp. salt
1 tsp. vanilla
2 cups Chips
¼ to ½ cup Topper

WHAT YOU DO
1. Preheat oven to 350°F. Line a 15×10-inch baking pan with foil, extending foil over edges. Cover bottom of prepared pan with Crackers, breaking to fit or overlapping as needed.
2. In a medium saucepan combine butter, brown sugar, Spice, and salt; bring to boiling, stirring to melt butter. Boil gently, without stirring, 2 minutes. Remove from heat. Stir in vanilla.
3. Spread butter mixture over Crackers. Bake 8 to 10 minutes or until bubbly. Place pan on a wire rack. Sprinkle with Chips; let stand 5 minutes to soften.
4. Spread Chips over crackers and sprinkle with Topper. Cool 30 minutes. Chill 1 hour or until chocolate is set. Using foil, lift out uncut candy. Break into irregular pieces. Makes 24 servings.

Crackers (pick one)
50 almond-nut rice crackers
11 to 12 graham cracker rectangles or 24 gluten-free graham cracker squares
30 pretzel crisp crackers
30 rich round or rectangular crackers
40 saltine crackers
40 round wheat crackers (Toasteds)

Spice (pick one)
Apple pie spice
Ground cinnamon
Ground ginger
Jamaican jerk seasoning
Pumpkin pie spice

Chips (pick one)
Bittersweet chocolate chips
Milk chocolate chips
Semisweet chocolate chips
White baking chips

Topper (pick one)
Almond toffee bits
Dried tart cherries, cranberries, or apricots, chopped
Red, white, and green sprinkles
Toasted pecans, peanuts, almonds, cashews, macadamia nuts, or walnuts, finely chopped

GRAHAM CRACKERS
+ BITTERSWEET
CHOCOLATE
+ DRIED CRANBERRIES
+ APRICOTS

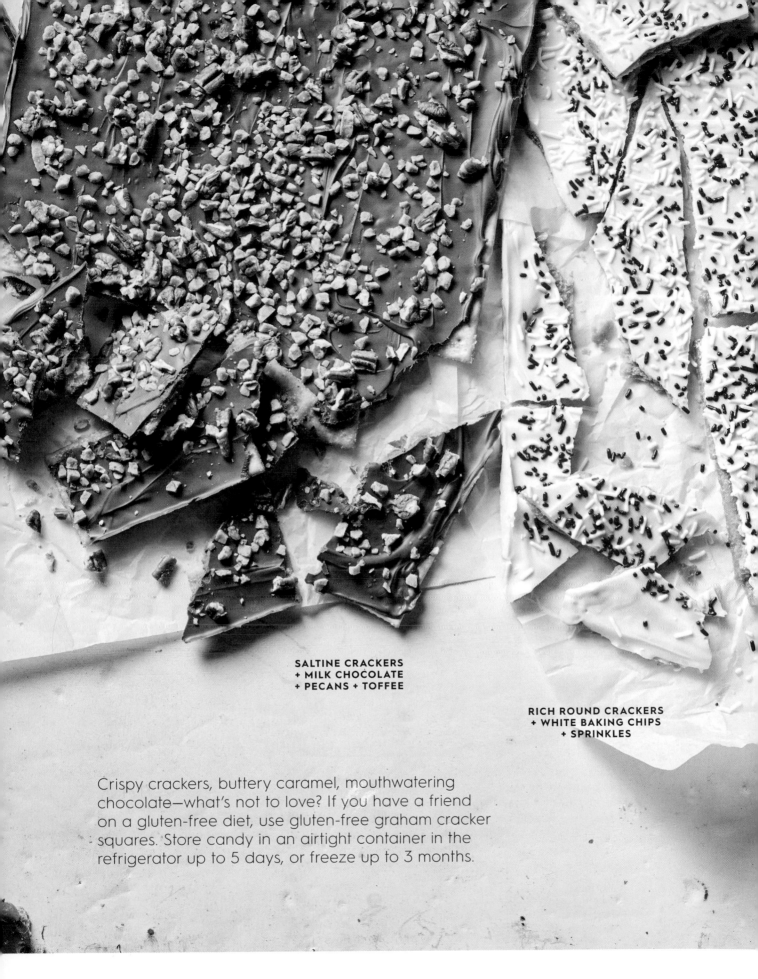

**SALTINE CRACKERS
+ MILK CHOCOLATE
+ PECANS + TOFFEE**

**RICH ROUND CRACKERS
+ WHITE BAKING CHIPS
+ SPRINKLES**

Crispy crackers, buttery caramel, mouthwatering
chocolate—what's not to love? If you have a friend
on a gluten-free diet, use gluten-free graham cracker
squares. Store candy in an airtight container in the
refrigerator up to 5 days, or freeze up to 3 months.

gifts

EXTEND JOY TO THOSE YOU LOVE
Let the merriment begin with
lovingly crafted gifts.

All Buttoned Up

Vintage or new, buttons lend an artistic touch to ordinary items just in time for the holiday season.

FLIP A LID

Whatever your recipient's favorite snack in a can, make it an unforgettable gift by crafting the unopened container into a reusable keepsake. Remove the plastic lid and place it top down on a cutting board. Using an awl, ice pick, or other pointed object, poke about a dozen holes randomly in the lid. Sew buttons to the lid through the holes, arranging and stacking as desired. Poke additional holes for buttons if needed. Wrap a strip of decorative paper around the can, piecing if needed. Use double-stick tape to secure the paper in place. Place on the lid for two gifts in one!

SIMPLY ELEGANT

No need for a bow when the ribbon is so beautifully embellished. Use embroidery floss to sew buttons onto ribbon, arranging in a cluster or a row. Wrap the gift with paper and top it off with the button-laden ribbon.

STITCH IT PRETTY

A large four-hole button is the crowning glory on this easy-to-make napkin ring. Starting with a flat-surface napkin ring, cut a piece of velvet ribbon to cover the ring with the ends slightly overlapping. Use a beading needle and thread to attach large seed beads every ½ inch along the long sides. Thread an embroidery needle with variegated floss. Leaving a 1-inch-long tail, insert the needle through one of the button holes from the backside. Thread on a large seed bead and insert the needle back through the same hole in the button. Continue in this manner until four seed beads have been secured to the button center. For each hole, bring the needle through the hole, around the button, and through the hole again. Continue working in this manner until each hole has three long stitches extending from the button holes around the outer rim of the button as shown. Bring the needle up through one of the button holes. Outline the center beads by weaving the floss through the long stitches in a pattern as desired. For the outer adornment, bring the thread to the button edge; thread on a large seed bead. Weave the floss under and over the spokes while adding beads, one within each spoke from the button hole and two between each spoke trio. Hot-glue the ribbon to the napkin ring and the large bead to the center.

PRETTY ASSORTMENT

Create miniature works of art using an eclectic mix of old and new buttons. Hot-glue buttons, single and stacked, to the top of a jar lid. Fill in any open areas with large and small beads. Cut a piece of cording long enough to encircle the lid plus 6 inches. Hot-glue the center of the cording to the top center of the ornament. Working with one side at a time, hot-glue the tails to the lid edge until they meet in the center at the bottom of the ornament. Knot the cording tails close to the ornament; trim and fray. For the hanger, cut a 12-inch-long piece of ribbon and knot the ends together. Hot-glue the knot to the top of the ornament.

Wondrous Weavings

Transform dollar-store finds into one-of-a-kind gifts using super-simple weaving patterns and fibers of your choosing.

PRETTY PAIL

Holiday treats are always welcome, but deliver them in a reusable woven bucket, and that's twice as nice! Choose an open-weave metal bucket to allow for weaving. Thread a large-eyed embroidery needle with yarn and weave it through the metal mesh in the desired pattern. Knot or hot-glue yarn ends to the inside of the bucket.

DESKTOP DUO

Personalize wire-mesh containers with all your gift recipient's favorite colors. Jute, string, leather cord, yarn, embroidery floss, and more can be used to bring color and distinction to the mesh surface. Weave fibers through the mesh in the desired repetitive pattern, using an embroidery needle if needed. Knot or use hot glue to secure the fiber ends to the inside of each container.

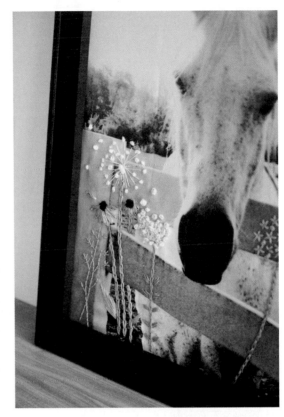

BASKET WEAVE

Choose any wire basket with a grid framework. Select four contrasting colors of chunky yarn. Make two upside-down V shapes. Knot the ends on the inside of the basket. Thread the remaining colors in a V shape, weaving through the other two colors in a simple under/over fashion.

FINISHING FEATURE

Contrasting colors, textures, and a corner tassel dress up this wire basket. Start with blue cord along the bottom at the right-hand corner. Make a knot about 2 inches from the end and unravel to create the tassel. Weave the blue around the basket twice to create two layers, then switch to the other colors.

Food Gifts

Share your appreciation of others with homemade cookies, candy, quick bread, and treats for the pup, all beautifully wrapped.

TOASTED COCONUT AND
CHOCOLATE CHIP SCONES

STITCHES ALL AROUND

Share scones with family and friends served on festive paper plates edged with pretty fibers. Use a pen and ruler to mark every inch along the rim of a decorative 9×9-inch paper plate, approximately ¼ inch from the edge. Hole-punch each dot. Thread a large-eyed embroidery needle with a pair of 36-inch long fibers to complement the design on the plate. Tape the ends to the back of the plate. Bring the needle up through the nearest hole, around the edge, and back up through the adjacent hole. Continue stitching in this manner until the entire border is stitched. Cut the tails and tape to the back of the plate. Accent the serving piece with a ribbon bow, adhered in place with double-sided tape.

TOASTED COCONUT AND CHOCOLATE CHIP SCONES

HANDS-ON TIME 20 minutes
BAKE 18 minutes at 400°F

WHAT YOU NEED

1 cup shredded unsweetened coconut
2¼ cups all-purpose flour
1 Tbsp. sugar
1 Tbsp. baking powder
¼ tsp. salt
6 Tbsp. cold butter
1 egg, lightly beaten
¾ cup heavy cream
1 cup semisweet chocolate chips
   Heavy cream

WHAT YOU DO

1. Preheat oven to 400°F. Spread coconut on a baking sheet; bake 5 to 7 minutes or until golden, stirring once. Cool slightly. Transfer to a food processor. Process until finely ground; set aside.

2. In a large bowl combine flour, sugar, baking powder, and salt. Using a pastry blender, cut in butter until mixture resembles course crumbs. Make a well in the center of the flour mixture.

3. In a medium bowl combine egg and the ¾ cup cream. Add egg mixture all at once to flour mixture. Add coconut and chocolate chips. Using a fork, stir just until moistened.

4. Turn dough out onto a lightly floured surface. Knead dough by folding and gently pressing for 10 to 12 strokes or until dough is nearly smooth. Pat dough into a 10×4-inch rectangle. Cut in half lengthwise then in sixths crosswise to make 12 rectangles.

5. Place rectangles 2 inches apart on an ungreased baking sheet. Brush wedges with additional cream. Bake 13 to 15 minutes or until golden brown. Sprinkle scones with additional shredded coconut the last 5 minutes of baking. Serve warm. Makes 12 servings.

PUMPKIN SPICED SPRITZ

WRAP 'N' ROLL

Whether gifting a handful or enough for a family, this pretty presentation makes your cookie delivery that much more special. For each end tie, thread a chenille stem with a jingle bell (or bells) and slide to the center; twist to secure. Choose two ¼-inch-wide ribbons and tie bows next to the bells. Stack the cookies and wrap, cracker-style, in decorative cellophane. Twist a chenille-stem tie on each end; trim ends short.

PUMPKIN SPICED SPRITZ

HANDS-ON TIME 20 minutes
BAKE 6 minutes per batch at 375°F

WHAT YOU NEED

1½ cups butter, softened
1 cup packed brown sugar
2 tsp. pumpkin pie spice
1 tsp. baking powder
¼ tsp. baking soda
¼ tsp. salt
¼ cup canned pumpkin
1 egg
1 tsp. vanilla
3½ cups all-purpose flour
¼ cup granulated sugar
2 tsp. pumpkin pie spice
¼ cup butter, melted

WHAT YOU DO

1. Preheat oven to 375°F. In a large bowl beat the 1½ cups butter with a mixer on medium to high 30 seconds. Add the next five ingredients (through salt). Beat until combined, scraping bowl as needed. Beat in pumpkin, egg, and vanilla until combined. Beat in flour.

2. Force unchilled dough through a cookie press 1 inch apart onto an ungreased cookie sheet. Bake 6 minutes or until edges are firm. Cool on a wire rack.

3. In a small bowl combine granulated sugar and 2 tsp. pumpkin spice. Dip tops of cookies into melted butter, then into sugar mixture to coat. Let stand until set. Makes 90 servings.

TOFFEE-PECAN COOKIE MIX

START TO FINISH 15 minutes

WHAT YOU NEED

1⅓ cups all-purpose flour
⅓ cup packed brown sugar
⅓ cup granulated sugar
½ tsp. baking soda
½ tsp. cream of tartar
¼ tsp. salt
⅔ cup bittersweet or semisweet chocolate chips
½ cup almond toffee bits
½ cup coconut
⅓ cup chopped toasted pecans

WHAT YOU DO

1. In a 1-qt. jar layer all of the ingredients. Store in a cool, dry place up to 1 month. Include directions for making cookies with gift. Makes 30 servings.

To Make Cookies Preheat oven to 350°F. Pour mix into a large bowl. Stir in 1 egg and ¼ cup each softened butter and vegetable oil until combined. Drop dough by teaspoons 2 inches apart onto an ungreased cookie sheet. Bake 8 to 10 minutes or until edges are lightly browned. Cool on cookie sheet 1 minute. Remove; cool on a wire rack. Makes about 30 cookies.

Milk Chocolate-Cherry Cookie Mix Prepare as directed, except use milk chocolate chips in place of the bittersweet chocolate chips and chopped dried cherries or cranberries in place of the almond toffee bits.

CANDY BAR BARK

HANDS-ON TIME 20 minutes
CHILL 30 minutes

WHAT YOU NEED

6 oz. chocolate- or vanilla-flavor candy coating (almond bark), chopped
6 oz. milk, semisweet, or dark chocolate, chopped, or white baking chips
1 Tbsp. shortening
1 cup chopped assorted candy bars
½ cup chopped toasted pecans, walnuts, or almonds

WHAT YOU DO

1. Line a large baking sheet with heavy foil; grease foil. In a large glass bowl combine candy coating, chocolate,

TOFFEE-PECAN COOKIE MIX

PUT A LID ON IT

Let your gift recipients enjoy baking fun by providing the cookie ingredients in a jolly jar that can be used long after the baking is done. To make polka-dot "snow" on the jar, dip a pencil eraser into etching cream and dot onto the jar surface. Follow the manufacturer's directions, wait the allotted time, then rinse off the etching cream. Wash and dry the jar. Place mix, in layers, in the jar. Trace around the jar lid onto white glitter paper; cut out. Hot-glue the paper to the lid. Create a scene on the lid using miniatures, such as trees, houses, and animals; hot-glue in place. Place the lid on the jar and tie a ribbon bow around the jar neck.

SUGAR COOKIE BARK

CANDY BAR BARK

and shortening. Microwave 1½ to 2 minutes or until chocolate is melted, stirring every 30 seconds.

2. Pour mixture onto prepared baking sheet and spread until ¼ inch thick. Sprinkle with candy bars and nuts. Chill 30 minutes or until firm. Break candy into pieces. Makes 36 servings.

Salted Caramel Bark Prepare and spread chocolate mixture as directed. In a medium glass bowl microwave half of a 14-oz. pkg. vanilla caramels, unwrapped, and 1 Tbsp. milk 1 to 2 minutes or until melted, stirring every 30 seconds. Drizzle chocolate mixture with melted caramels. Sprinkle with ¾ cup chopped toasted almonds and ¼ tsp. sea salt. Chill as directed.

Mint-Chocolate Bark Line baking sheet with foil; grease foil. Arrange 9 chocolate wafer cookies on prepared baking sheet. Using vanilla coating, melt half of the coating with 3 oz. milk chocolate chips and ½ Tbsp. of the shortening. Melt remaining coating with 3 oz. green mint-flavor baking chips. Drop alternating spoonfuls of chocolate and mint mixtures onto cookies. Using a narrow spatula, swirl mixtures. Sprinkle with chopped layered chocolate-mint candies. Chill as directed.

S'more Bark Using vanilla coating, prepare and spread as directed. Sprinkle with candy bars. Top with tiny marshmallows and coarsely crushed graham crackers. Chill as directed.

Sugar Cookie Bark Using vanilla coating, prepare and spread as directed. Sprinkle with crushed sugar cookies and red, white, and green sprinkles or jimmies. Chill as directed.

To Store Layer candy between waxed paper in an airtight container. Store in refrigerator up to 2 weeks.

TIMELY WRAP

A multitude of seasonal scrapbook papers awaits to personalize your candy gift-giving. For each sleeve, cut an 8½-inch square from two-sided cardstock. Overlap two opposite points; secure with double-sided tape. Adorn the center with a dimensional decorative sticker. Wrap bark with clear cellophane, seal, and slip into sleeve.

CINNAMON CHURRO
SNACK MIX

CAN TO THE RESCUE

Recycle a soup-size can by making it into a stylish container. Cut one 4×11-inch or two 2½×11-inch pieces of ribbon to cover can; hot-glue in place, overlapping as needed. Cut two 18-inch pieces of ⅜-inch-wide ribbon. Hot-glue the center of each ribbon to the back of the can. Bring the ribbons to the front and tie into bows; trim ribbon ends. Hot-glue cord around top edge of can. Place snack mix in a cellophane bag before inserting into the can; tie bag closed with ribbon.

CINNAMON CHURRO SNACK MIX

HANDS-ON TIME 20 minutes
BAKE 20 minutes at 325°F

WHAT YOU NEED

- 2 cups bite-size corn square cereal
- 2 cups bite-size rice square cereal
- 2 cups mini pretzel twists
- 2 cups horn-shape crisp corn snack (Bugles), plain mini bagel chips, or bite-size wheat square cereal
- 2 cups pecan halves or cashews
- ½ cup granulated sugar
- 2 tsp. ground cinnamon
- ⅔ cup butter, cut up
- ⅔ cup packed brown sugar
- ½ tsp. vanilla

WHAT YOU DO

1. Preheat oven to 325°F. Line a shallow roasting pan with foil, extending foil over edges. In prepared pan combine the first five ingredients (through pecans). In a small bowl stir together granulated sugar and cinnamon.

2. In a medium saucepan cook and stir butter and brown sugar over medium until sugar is dissolved and mixture is smooth. Stir in vanilla.

3. Drizzle cereal mixture with butter mixture; toss to coat. Sprinkle with half of the cinnamon-sugar; toss to coat. Sprinkle with remaining cinnamon-sugar; toss again.

4. Bake 10 minutes; stir. Bake 10 minutes more. Use foil to lift snack mix from pan; cool on foil. Store in an airtight container at room temperature up to 1 week. Makes 24 servings.

SALTED NUT TRUFFLES

HANDS-ON TIME 45 minutes
MICROWAVE 2 minutes
STAND 30 minutes

WHAT YOU NEED

- 1 7-oz. jar marshmallow creme
- 1 cup creamy peanut butter
- 1 cup powdered sugar
- ¾ cup lightly salted cocktail peanuts, finely chopped
- 2 Tbsp. light-color corn syrup
- 2 cups white baking pieces or milk chocolate pieces
- 1 Tbsp. shortening
  Finely chopped cocktail peanuts and/or decorating sugar (optional)

WHAT YOU DO

1. Line a baking sheet or tray with waxed paper. In a large microwave-safe bowl combine marshmallow creme and peanut butter. Heat, uncovered, on high 30 seconds or until mixture is slightly softened; stirring once. Stir in powdered sugar, the ¾ cup finely chopped peanuts, and the corn syrup until well combined.

2. Shape the peanut butter mixture into 1-inch balls. Place balls on the prepared baking sheet.

3. In a small microwave-safe bowl heat white baking pieces or milk chocolate pieces and shortening, uncovered, on medium 2 minutes or until pieces are melted, stirring twice.

4. Using a fork, dip balls into melted coating, allowing excess mixture to drip back into bowl. Return balls to prepared baking sheet. If using, sprinkle truffles with additional finely chopped peanuts, decorating sugar, and/or drizzle with additional melted coating. Let stand 30 minutes or until set. If necessary, chill to set. Makes 56 servings.

GETTING IN SHAPE

Wrapping-paper scraps dress up plain cardboard triangles, transforming them into holiday-ready serving trays. Using the patterns on page 156, cut each from lightweight cardboard. Lightly score the lines along the edge of the larger triangle. Wrap the triangle, taping the edges to the center. Cut out the notches in the corners; fold up and secure with clear tape. (Note: Any uncovered area in the center will be covered by the liner.) Wrap the smaller triangle with paper; tape edges to the back. Place the liner in the tray. Hot-glue a decorative sticker or small decoration to one tip of the triangle. Place truffles in mini paper liners and arrange on the tray.

SALTED NUT TRUFFLES

HUMMINGBIRD
BREAD

WREATH INSPIRED

Arrange slices of bread in a circle on a large plate or charger. Cut a 36-inch length from 2½-inch-wide ribbon. Tie a bow in the center. Hot-glue a trio of white-edged pinecones to the center of the bow. Use double-sided tape to adhere the bow to the outer rim of the plate.

HUMMINGBIRD BREAD

HANDS-ON TIME 20 minutes
BAKE 1 hour at 350°F
COOL 10 minutes

WHAT YOU NEED

2	cups all-purpose flour
2	tsp. baking powder
1	tsp. ground cinnamon
½	tsp. baking soda
½	tsp. salt
¼	tsp. ground allspice
1	8-oz. can crushed pineapple, drained
1	cup mashed overripe bananas (2 to 3)
1	cup sugar
½	cup vegetable oil
2	eggs, lightly beaten
1	tsp. vanilla
½	cup shredded or flaked coconut
¼	cup chopped toasted pecans
1	recipe Cream Cheese Drizzle

WHAT YOU DO

1. Preheat oven to 350°F. Grease bottom and ½ inch up sides of a 9×5-inch loaf pan. In a large bowl stir together the first six ingredients (through allspice). Make a well in the center of flour mixture.

2. In a medium bowl combine the next six ingredients (through vanilla). Add pineapple mixture all at once to flour mixture. Stir just until moistened. Fold in coconut and pecans. Transfer batter to prepared loaf pan.

3. Bake 1 hour or until a toothpick comes out clean. Cool in pan on a wire rack 10 minutes. Remove from pan; cool completely. Drizzle with Cream Cheese Drizzle. If desired, sprinkle with additional coconut and pecans. Makes 10 servings.

Cream Cheese Drizzle In a small bowl combine 1 oz. cream cheese, softened, and 1 Tbsp. butter, softened, until smooth. Stir in ½ cup powdered sugar and enough milk (about 1 Tbsp.) to reach drizzling consistency.

CARROT AND PEANUT BUTTER PUP CAKES

DOGGONE CLEVER

Craft bone-shape trays to deliver treats to favorite pooches. Trace the bone pattern on page 156; cut out the shape. Use the pattern to cut two bone shapes from lightweight cardboard. Cut a 1½×26-inch strip from decorative cardstock, piecing as needed by taping seams on the back. Draw a guideline ¼ inch from the edge along one long side of the strip. Using fringing scissors, cut in ¼ inch, stopping at the drawn line. Press the fringe under and tape it to one of the bone shapes, leaving a ⅛-inch border. (If you don't have fringing scissors, use regular scissors to make snips along the edge approximately ¼ inch apart.) Overlap the ends; tape in place. Hot-glue trim around the base. Trim ⅛ inch from the edge of the second bone shape. Line the bone container with the bone shape and paper shred. Arrange Pup Cakes in the tray and slip into a cellophane bag before gifting.

CARROT AND PEANUT BUTTER PUP CAKES

HANDS-ON TIME 15 minutes
BAKE 12 minutes at 350°F
COOL 10 minutes

WHAT YOU NEED

1¾	cups white whole wheat flour
1	tsp. baking powder
2	eggs
¾	cup shredded carrots
½	cup natural creamy peanut butter
⅓	cup unsweetened applesauce
¼	cup honey
1	Tbsp. canola oil
1	cup natural apple juice
½	cup natural creamy peanut butter (optional)
3	oz. cream cheese, softened (optional)

WHAT YOU DO

1. Preheat oven to 350°F. Grease and flour forty-eight 1¾-inch muffin cups or line with paper bake cups. In a medium bowl stir together flour and baking powder.

2. In a large bowl beat the next six ingredients (through oil) with a mixer on low to medium until combined. Add flour mixture and apple juice alternately, beating on low after each addition until combined. Divide batter among prepared muffin cups.

3. Bake 12 to 15 minutes or until a toothpick comes out clean. Cool in muffin cups on wire racks 10 minutes. Remove from cups; cool on wire racks.

4. If using frosting, in a small bowl beat ½ cup peanut butter and the cream cheese on medium until combined. Using a decorating bag fitted with a large star tip, pipe a star onto each pup cake. Makes 48 servings.

To Store Store in refrigerator up to 1 week.

Flakes of Felt

WINTRY COASTERS

Craft a set of wintry coasters in mere minutes, using crafts-store felt snowflakes. Use fabric glue to attach a 4- to 5-inch felt snowflake to contrasting felt; let dry. Use pinking shears to trim around the snowflake, leaving a narrow border.

SNOW-CUTE TAG

Craft dimensional gift tags using felt snowflakes and jingle bells adorning layers of pretty papers. Cut a 2½×4½-inch piece of white cardstock. Top with one or two additional papers cut in graduating rectangles, adhering with a glue stick. Use a paper punch to make a hole at one end; thread with ribbon. Hot-glue snippets from a felt snowflake and jingle bells on the left side of the tag. Use a marking pen to write the recipient's name in the open space.

ENCHANTING BOX TOP

Some gifts are just too special for ordinary wraps. Here's a quick way to make that gift stand out from the rest. Wrap a plain box and lid with pretty craft or wrapping papers. Hot-glue a felt snowflake to the center of the lid. Top with a plastic snowflake, large jingle bell, and faux bird perched on top.

ADORNED RIBBON

Bows are beautiful, but this package topper is unforgettable. Using a jar, cup, or other round object, trace a circle slightly larger than the felt snowflake onto contrasting felt. Cut out the circle using pinking shears. Thread ribbon through holes in the snowflake center; use hot glue to attach the circle to the back. Wrap the embellishment around the package; hot-glue in place.

kids

GET READY FOR WINTERTIME CRAFTS
Have fun making decorations, greetings, gifts, and wraps as magical as Santa and his reindeer.

On the Fringe

Yarn fringes add fun accents to holiday trims. Master the technique and use them to give personality to all sorts of paper decorations.

JOLLY OL' ELF

Hanging from an evergreen branch or trimming the top of a wrapped gift, St. Nick is always a welcome face during the holiday season.

WHAT YOU NEED
Tracing paper
Pencil
Scissors
Scrapbook papers in red print and tan
Fine black marking pen
Toothpick
White acrylic paint
Glue stick
¼-inch-wide ribbon to complement
    hat paper
⅛-inch paper punch
White yarn
Hot-glue gun; glue sticks
Red yarn

WHAT YOU DO
1. Trace the hat and face patterns from page 158 onto tracing paper; cut out. Use the patterns to cut the hat shape from red print paper and the face from tan paper.
2. Draw in the eyes with a black fine marking pen. For the left eye highlight, dip a toothpick into white paint and dot onto the eye as shown. Let the paint dry.
3. Adhere the hat to the top of the head using a glue stick. Cut two lengths of ¼-inch-wide ribbon for the hat band; glue in place folding the ends to the back.
4. Use paper punch to punch a hole at the top of the hat for hanging and one near the tip of the hat. Cut three 6-inch pieces of white yarn. Fold each piece of yarn in half. Working with one at a time, poke yarn loop through the hole from the back. Thread the yarn ends through the loop; pull snug.
5. Punch a row of holes across the lower portion of the face piece, leaving approximately ¼ inch between holes. For each beard fringe, cut a 6-inch piece of white yarn; fold in half. Thread the loop

through the face piece from the back. Thread the yarn ends through the loop; pull snug. Trim the yarn into a beard shape, shorter at the sides and longer toward the bottom.
6. Cut two ¾-inch pieces of yarn, glue over eyes on hat brim for eyebrows. For the mustache, cut fourteen 4-inch pieces of yarn. Lay the strands together, aligning

the ends. Use one of the strands to tie a knot in the center of the bundle. Hot-glue the center of the mustache to the face, asking an adult for help if needed.
7. For hanger, cut a 12-inch piece of yarn; fold in half. Thread the loop through the back of the hole in the hat and pull the yarn ends through the loop; pull snug. Knot the yarn tails together.

ON THE CUFF

Merry and mini, these stocking ornaments are easy to make from fun holiday prints and yarn. Trace the stocking pattern on page 158 onto tracing paper; cut out. Use the pattern to cut a shape from holiday cardstock. Cut a 1×3½-inch piece of cardstock for the cuff. Use a paper punch to punch a row of holes across the center of the strip, leaving approximately ⅛ inch between holes. For each fringe, cut a 6-inch piece of yarn; fold in half. Thread the loop through a hole in the cuff piece from the back. Thread the yarn ends through the loop; pull snug. Glue the top of the cuff to the stocking. Add a yarn hanging loop through the right hole in the cuff.

BOX TOP

Recycle small boxes into holiday favors you'll be proud to give. If the box has flaps, cut those off the top (ask an adult for help if needed). Cover the box sides with holiday scrapbook paper or wrapping paper, folding over ¼ inch of paper to the inside; tape in place. Using a paper punch, make holes along the top, ¼-inch from the top and ½ inch apart. For each fringe, cut a 6-inch piece of yarn. Fold the yarn in half and thread the loop through one of the holes from the inside of the box. Thread the yarn ends through the loop and pull snug. Trim the yarn tails to approximately ½ inches long.

TRIM THE TREE

A handmade holiday card sends a great big message of love. To make a card, trace and cut out the pattern on page 158. Use the pattern to cut a tree shape from holiday cardstock. Hole-punch along the bottom edge, approximately ¼ inch from the edge and leaving ¼ inch between holes. For fringe, cut enough 6-inch pieces of yarn to fill the holes. Working one fringe at a time, fold the yarn in half. Thread the loop through the tree from the back of a hole, insert the ends into the loop, and pull snug. Continue until all fringes are complete. Use a glue stick to adhere the tree to a 4½×6½-inch piece of white cardstock. Glue it atop green paper; trim a narrow border. Adhere the design to a 5×7-inch blank card front. Tie a bow using four strands of yarn; hot-glue to the treetop.

LOOSE ENDS

Surprise all your favorite people with clever "cracker-style" rolls filled with candy. For each roll, cut a 5×6-inch piece of holiday cardstock. Hole-punch each short end, approximately ½ inch apart. For each fringe, cut a 6-inch piece of yarn. Fold the yarn in half; thread the loop through a hole from the back. Thread the loose ends through the loop; pull snug. Continue until all fringes are complete. Shape the paper into a roll; overlap ends and tape to secure. Accent the center with ribbons; hot-glue ends in place. Tuck a cellophane bag into the roll; fill with small candies. Cut two 4-inch-long pieces of yarn and use them to tie up each end of roll.

TOP IT OFF

Handcrafted bows make gifts all that more meaningful. To make one, trace around a round object onto print cardstock; cut out. Make a series of evenly spaced holes around the circle edge using a paper punch. For each fringe, cut two 6-inch pieces of yarn. Fold the yarn in half; thread the folded ends through a hole from the back. Thread the loose ends through the loops; pull snug. Once fringes are in place, trim the ends even. To make the center pom-pom, wrap the tines of a fork with yarn approximately 20 times. Thread a 12-inch piece of yarn between the center; tie tight. Slip yarn off the fork and cut the loops. Using an awl or ice pick, poke a pair of holes near the center of the circle. Thread a yarn end from the pom-pom through each hole. Tie the yarn ends into a knot to secure.

Kids on a Roll

Save cardboard rolls from the recycling bin and use them to print one-of-a-kind seasonal place mats and wrapping supplies.

SNOWMAN GREETINGS

This happy fellow is sure to pass on the spirit of the season!

WHAT YOU NEED
Cardboard tubes in two slightly different sizes
White acrylic paint
Scrap of paper
Scraps of cardboard
Blank colored 4×6-inch notecards
Straws in two sizes

WHAT YOU DO
1. Place some white paint on a paper scrap and smooth with a piece of cardboard as shown in Photo A.
2. For the body, dip the larger tube into white paint and press onto the bottom of a notecard as shown in Photo B. Use the smaller tube to print the head as shown in Photo C.
3. To make the scarf, flatten the smaller tube, pinching one end to make a paisley shape. Print two shapes between the head and body as shown in Photo D.
4. For the hat, cut a 1¼-inch piece of cardboard; dip it into paint. Press the straight piece at the top of the head at an angle as shown in Photo E. Cut a 1-inch piece of cardboard; dip into paint. Add 5 lines above the first one, keeping centered as shown in Photo F.
5. To make the arms, cut a 2-inch piece of cardboard, dip in paint, and press onto body where desired as shown in Photo G. To add twig-looking hands, fold a 1-inch piece of cardboard in half, press into paint, and press near the ends of each arm line as shown in Photo H.
6. For the eyes, mouth, and buttons, dip a small straw into paint and dot onto the surface as shown in Photo I.
7. Use the larger straw to add a nose and snow as shown in Photo J. Let the paint dry.

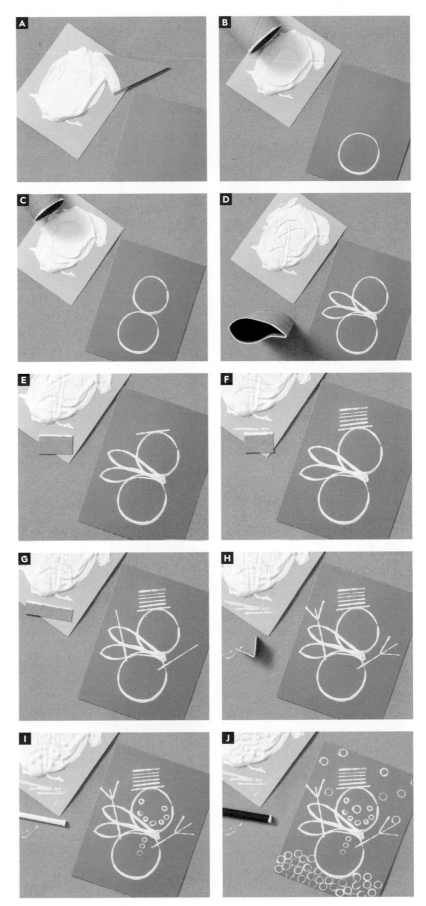

POINSETTIA WRAP

Even printer paper can become special wrapping paper with printed poinsettias gracing the surface. To create the petal stamp, flatten a short cardboard tube lengthwise as shown in Photo A. Dip the end of the tube into red paint and press onto the paper as shown in Photo B, adding as many petals as desired. Dip a pencil eraser into yellow paint and dot the flower center. Make as many poinsettias on the paper as desired. Let the paint dry.

ONE-OF-A-KIND GIFT TAGS

Use your big imagination to craft original snowflake gift tags that deliver mini messages of cheer. Start with small scraps of solid-color cardstock folded into squares. Use cardboard tubes, straws, and scraps of straight cardboard dipped into white paint to print a snowflake. Try to make the design somewhat symmetrical to resemble a snowflake. Let the paint dry.

MERRY PLACE MATS

Surprise your family with hand-printed place mats brightening up the table come mealtime. For a look like this one, start with a 12-inch square of scrapbook paper. Add contrasting stripes of paper; secure by taping on the back. Use your imagination for printing tools. The double rings shown here were made with an empty transparent tape roll, the large circles with a plastic cup, and the small circles with a straw. For an easier version, use heavy wrapping paper cut to size for the base. For longer-lasting place mats, have them laminated at a copy shop.

RINGS-ALL-AROUND GIFT BAGS

Make inexpensive gift bags with an easy print technique that takes just minutes. Use an empty transparent tape roll and dip into acrylic paint. Lay the closed bag flat on a work surface. Press the roll on the paper and carefully lift it. Reload the roll with paint before each print. If using more than one color, wash and dry the roll before changing paints. Let the paint dry.

Creative Snow Cones

COOKIE CUPS

Paper-punch holes on opposite sides of a snow cone cup. Thread a chenille stem through the holes; twist end around chenille stem to secure and shape into a handle. Hot-glue alternating red and white pom-poms around the rim. Glue a pom-pom to the tip. Place stickers on the front, and a message or to-and-from sticker on the handle.

SUPER-CUTE POP-OUT CARD

Once a blank photo card, this dimensional beauty will delight all your family and friends. Start with a 5½×7¼-inch solid-color card. To add a pretty backdrop for the tree, cut two 4×6-inch pieces of decorative paper—one white glitter and the other cutout snowflake. (Or, use a single layer of your choosing.) Adhere the layers together using a glue stick. Glue the accent papers to the center of the card. To make the tree, flatten a red-and-white snow cone cup. Using pinking shears, cut the cup into three pieces, rounding the cuts as shown. Use a strip of strong double-sided tape to adhere the overlapping cup pieces to the card where shown. Add a piece of ¼-inch-wide ribbon for the tree trunk. Accent the treetop and branches with stickers.

SNOWMAN ORNAMENT

To make a hanger, cut a 12-inch piece of yarn; knot the ends together. Snip off the very tip of one cup. Thread the folded end of yarn through the hole from the inside of the cup. Hot-glue a pom-pom to the tip. Place a 3½-inch foam ball into the cup. Secure the cup to the ball using pins poked through mini faux flowers. Add contrasting flowers and a bow to one side. For the face, poke a white map pin in the center of the foam ball for the nose. For the eyes, press the prongs of black paper fasteners into the foam. Add eye accents and a smile with black map pins. For the scarf, knot two 8-inch lengths of ribbon together; pin to bottom of foam ball.

TWO-CUP TRIM

Your Christmas tree will be merrier than ever with these big, bold ornaments gracing the branches. To make a hanger, cut a 12-inch piece of yarn; knot the ends together. Snip off the very tip of one cup. Thread the folded end of yarn through the hole from the inside of the cup. Thread a wooden bead on the yarn and slide onto the tip of the cup. Hot-glue a second cup to the first, opening to opening (ask an adult for help if needed). Hot-glue trim over the seam. Cut several pieces of ribbon; knot in the center. Trim the ribbon ends at an angle. Hot-glue the ribbons to the center of the top cup. Glue stickers, buttons, erasers, or other small decorations on and by the bow.

TREETOP CANDY COVER

Surprise family and friends with a cute striped tree covering a dish of sweet treats. To fringe the bottom of the cup, paper-punch holes approximately every ⅓ inch just above the snow cone rim. For the fringe, choose four colors of yarn as shown. Choose pairs of colors and use throughout the project. Cut two 6-inch pieces of yarn; fold in half. Thread the folded ends through one hole from the inside of the snow cone. Pull the yarn ends through the loop; pull snug. Once all fringes are in place, trim the fringes even, about 1 inch in length. Cut a 12-inch piece of each yarn color. Tie the yarn into one bow; hot-glue it to the tip of the cup. Use a small glass or cup on a stem to raise the tree from the plate. Fill the cup with candy and cover with the tree.

patterns

3-D PAPER SCULPTURES
pages 24–29
Enlarge patterns to
suggested sizes or your
desired sizes.

OAK LEAF

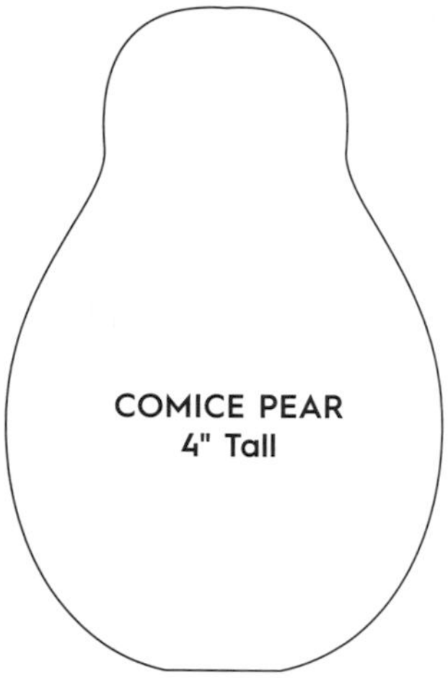

COMICE PEAR
4" Tall

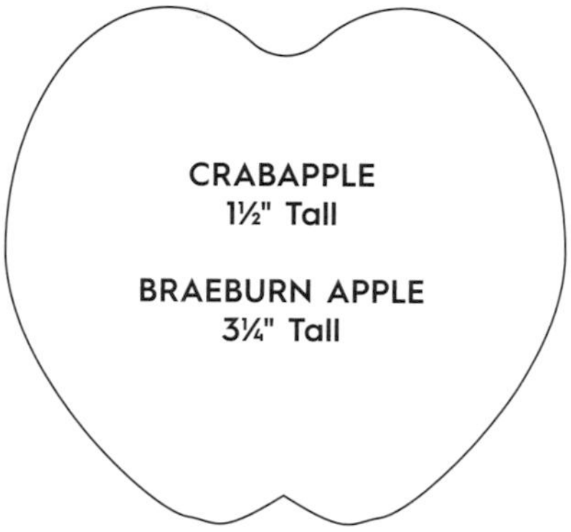

CRABAPPLE
1½" Tall

BRAEBURN APPLE
3¼" Tall

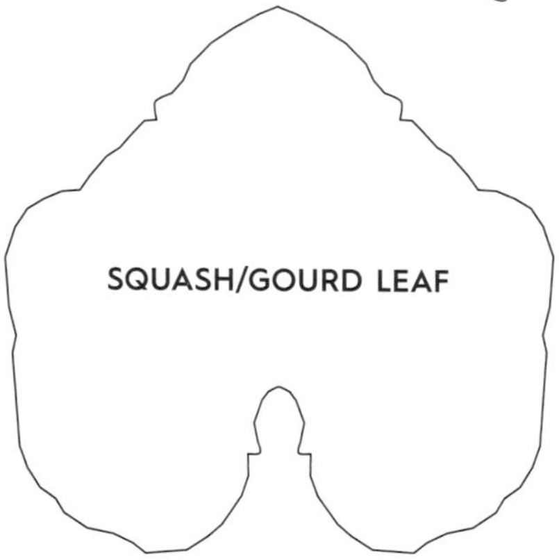

SQUASH/GOURD LEAF

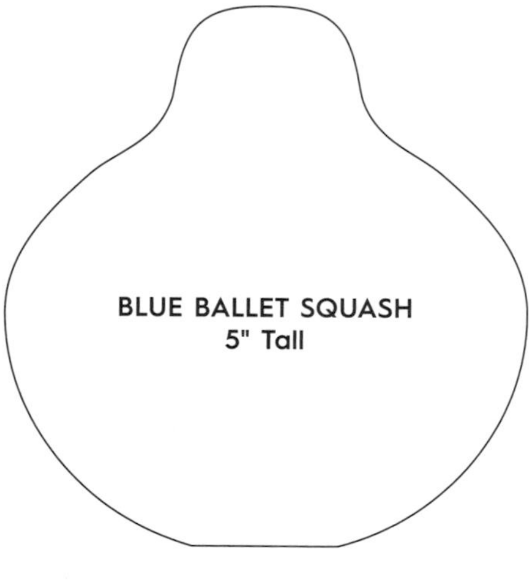

BLUE BALLET SQUASH
5" Tall

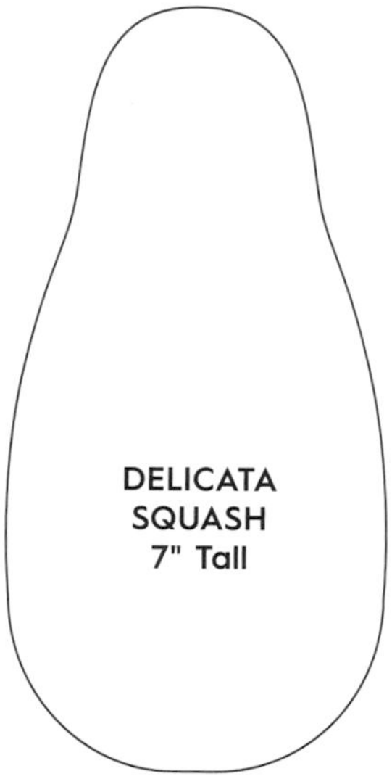

DELICATA
SQUASH
7" Tall

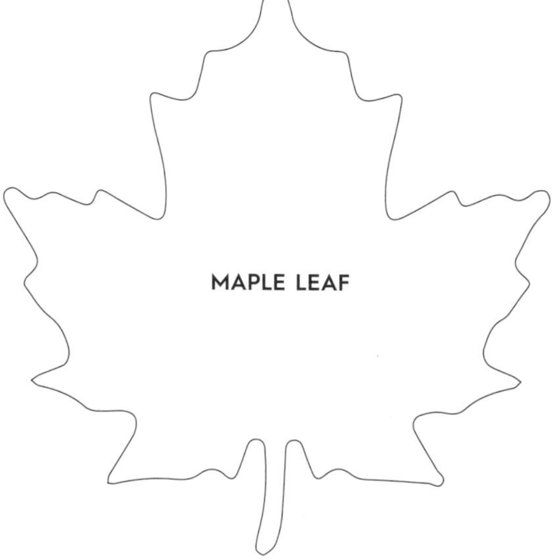

MAPLE LEAF

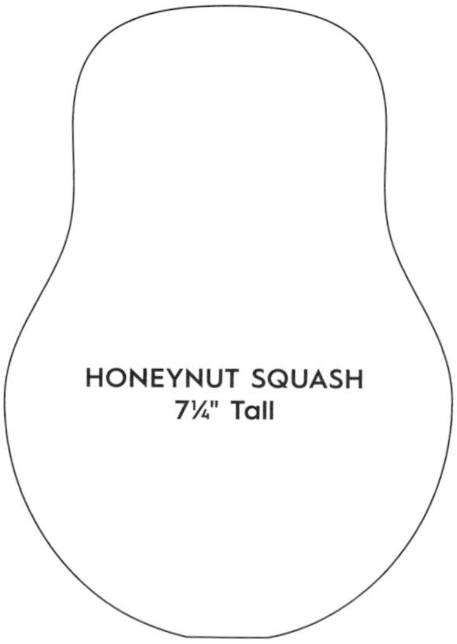

HONEYNUT SQUASH
7¼" Tall

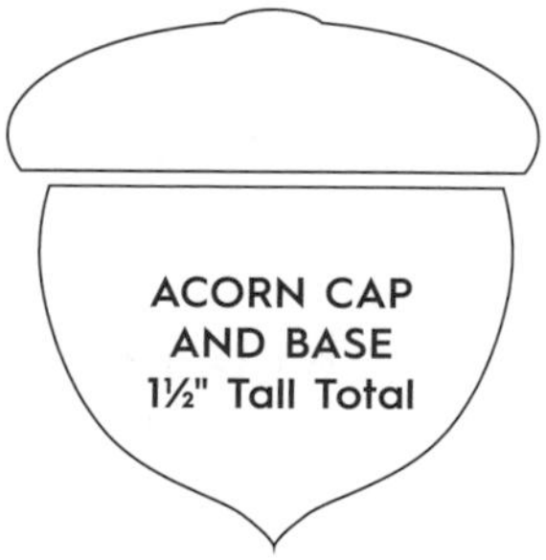

ACORN CAP
AND BASE
1½" Tall Total

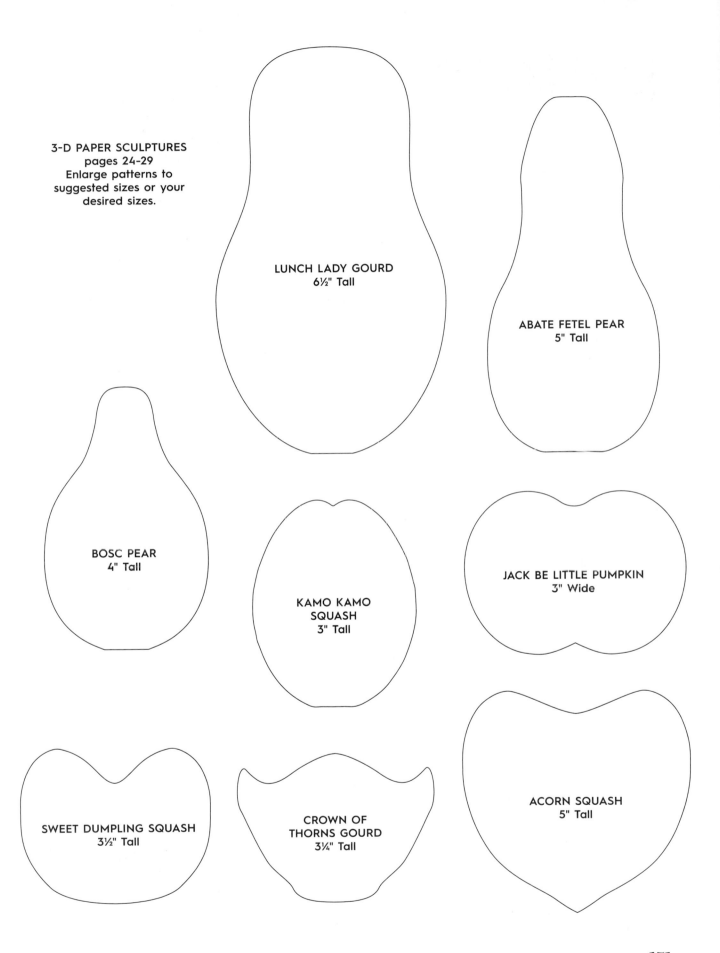

3-D PAPER SCULPTURES
pages 24-29
Enlarge patterns to
suggested sizes or your
desired sizes.

LUNCH LADY GOURD
6½" Tall

ABATE FETEL PEAR
5" Tall

BOSC PEAR
4" Tall

KAMO KAMO
SQUASH
3" Tall

JACK BE LITTLE PUMPKIN
3" Wide

SWEET DUMPLING SQUASH
3½" Tall

CROWN OF
THORNS GOURD
3¼" Tall

ACORN SQUASH
5" Tall

Patterns

LITTLE CRITTERS
Fox and Owl Pumpkin Patterns
page 31
Enlarge 200%

STAR OF WONDER
Card Star Pattern
page 73
Full-Size Pattern

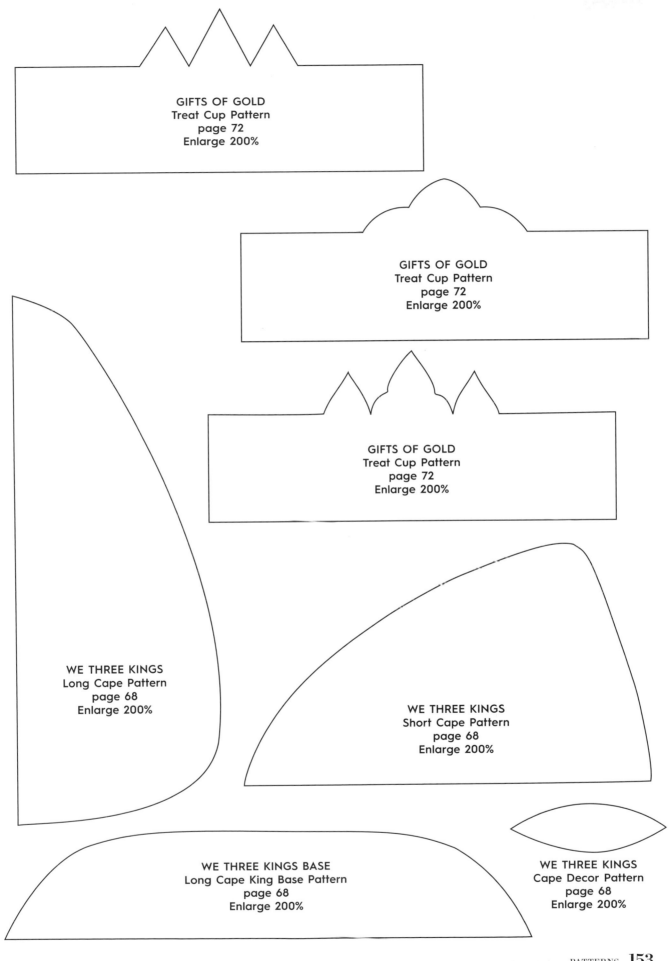

GIFTS OF GOLD
Treat Cup Pattern
page 72
Enlarge 200%

GIFTS OF GOLD
Treat Cup Pattern
page 72
Enlarge 200%

GIFTS OF GOLD
Treat Cup Pattern
page 72
Enlarge 200%

WE THREE KINGS
Long Cape Pattern
page 68
Enlarge 200%

WE THREE KINGS
Short Cape Pattern
page 68
Enlarge 200%

WE THREE KINGS BASE
Long Cape King Base Pattern
page 68
Enlarge 200%

WE THREE KINGS
Cape Decor Pattern
page 68
Enlarge 200%

Patterns

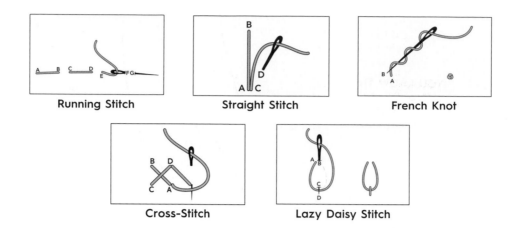

Running Stitch

Straight Stitch

French Knot

Cross-Stitch

Lazy Daisy Stitch

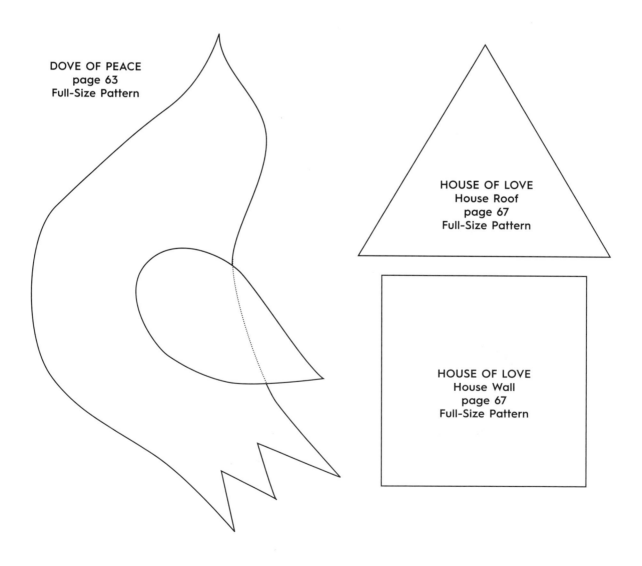

DOVE OF PEACE
page 63
Full-Size Pattern

HOUSE OF LOVE
House Roof
page 67
Full-Size Pattern

HOUSE OF LOVE
House Wall
page 67
Full-Size Pattern

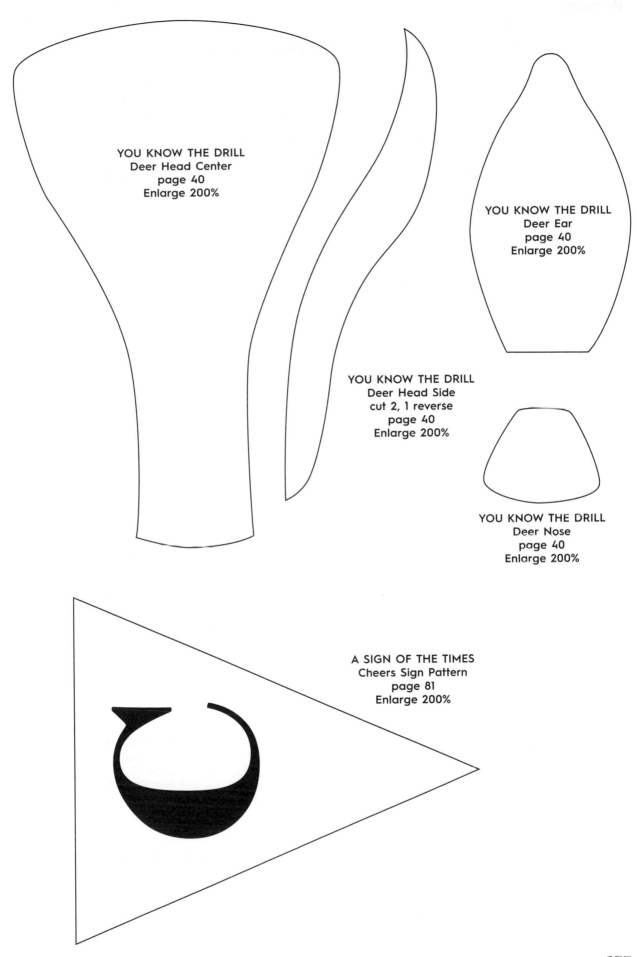

YOU KNOW THE DRILL
Deer Head Center
page 40
Enlarge 200%

YOU KNOW THE DRILL
Deer Ear
page 40
Enlarge 200%

YOU KNOW THE DRILL
Deer Head Side
cut 2, 1 reverse
page 40
Enlarge 200%

YOU KNOW THE DRILL
Deer Nose
page 40
Enlarge 200%

A SIGN OF THE TIMES
Cheers Sign Pattern
page 81
Enlarge 200%

Patterns

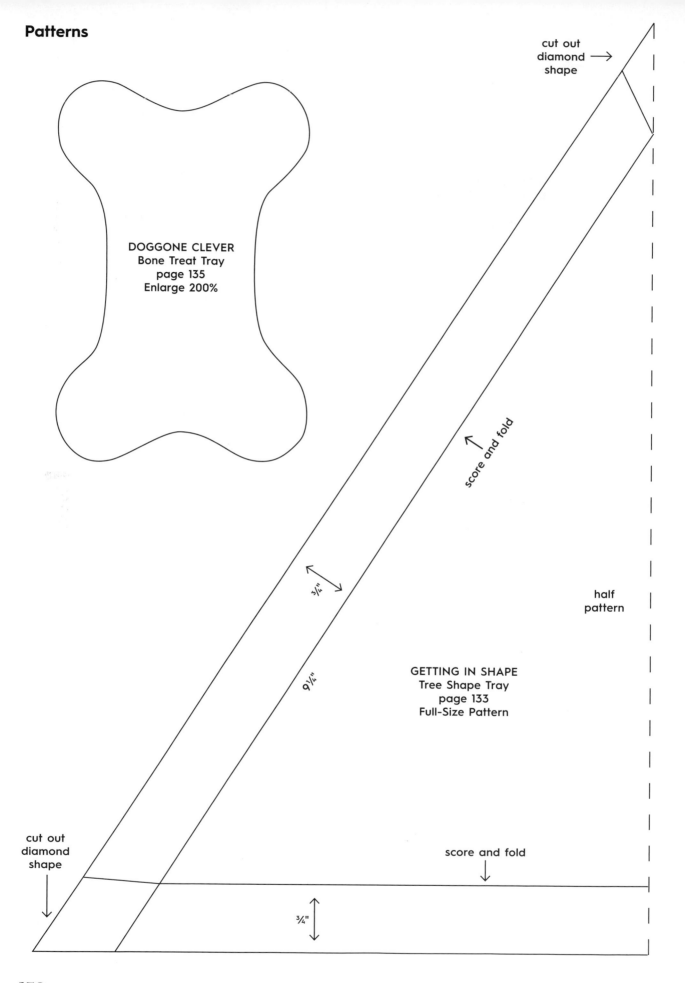

cut out
diamond
shape →

DOGGONE CLEVER
Bone Treat Tray
page 135
Enlarge 200%

score and fold

¾"

9½"

half
pattern

GETTING IN SHAPE
Tree Shape Tray
page 133
Full-Size Pattern

cut out
diamond
shape

score and fold

¾"

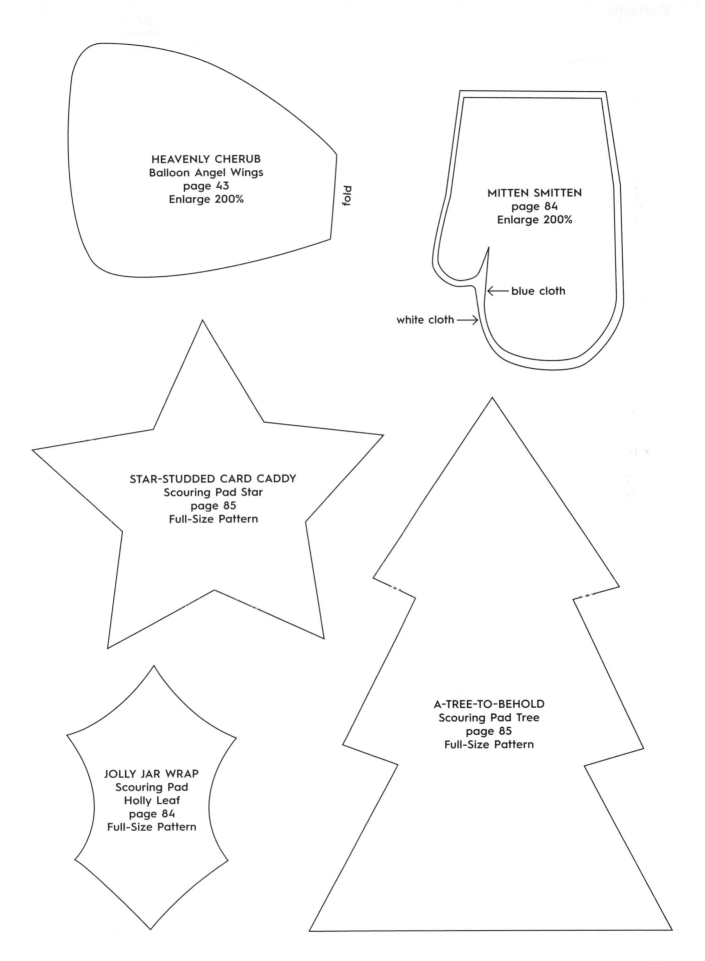

HEAVENLY CHERUB
Balloon Angel Wings
page 43
Enlarge 200%

fold

MITTEN SMITTEN
page 84
Enlarge 200%

← blue cloth

white cloth →

STAR-STUDDED CARD CADDY
Scouring Pad Star
page 85
Full-Size Pattern

A-TREE-TO-BEHOLD
Scouring Pad Tree
page 85
Full-Size Pattern

JOLLY JAR WRAP
Scouring Pad
Holly Leaf
page 84
Full-Size Pattern

Patterns

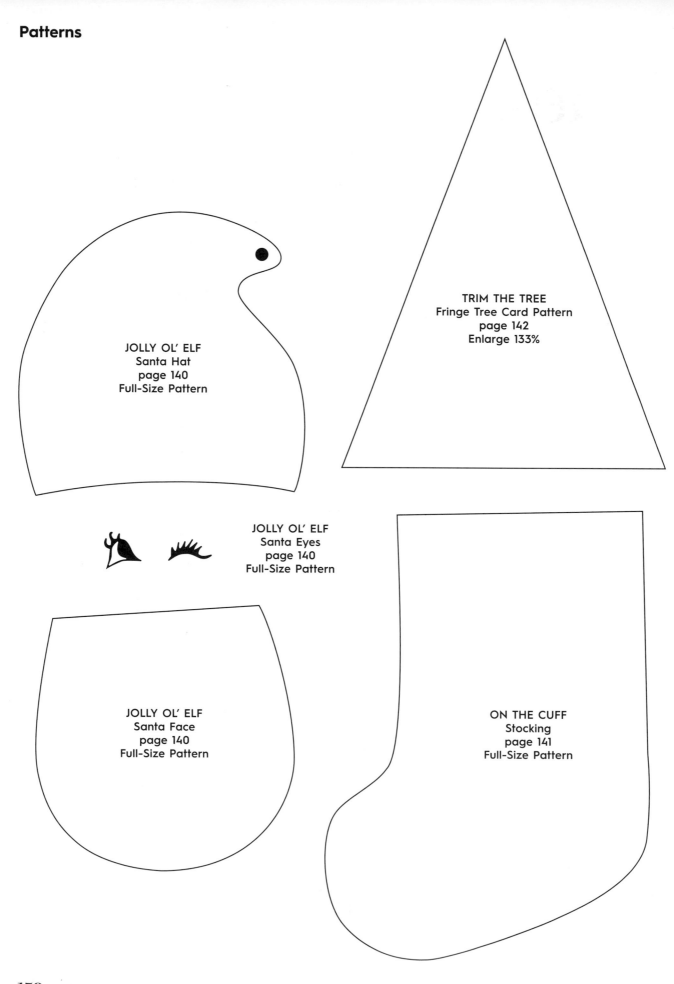

JOLLY OL' ELF
Santa Hat
page 140
Full-Size Pattern

TRIM THE TREE
Fringe Tree Card Pattern
page 142
Enlarge 133%

JOLLY OL' ELF
Santa Eyes
page 140
Full-Size Pattern

JOLLY OL' ELF
Santa Face
page 140
Full-Size Pattern

ON THE CUFF
Stocking
page 141
Full-Size Pattern

index